D1715278

DETAILS

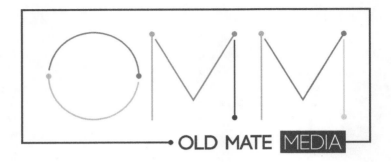

First Published in 2020 by Old Mate Media.

Written and Edited by: Chris Stead
Designed by: Chris Stead
Published by: Old Mate Media
ISBN: 978-1-925638-74-5

First Edition

CONTENTS

Type the genius links into a browser to buy products

INTRODUCTION

Children love Nintendo. It's been that way ever since a moustachioed little plumber first climbed his way up the scaffolding around a tall tower to rescue a princess from the grasp of a giant monkey. Mario, Princess Peach and Donkey Kong would just be the start, of course. For the best of 40-years now, Nintendo has continued to deliver the most beloved characters and game worlds we've ever seen.

While it's slightly changed in recent years with the arrival of some Nintendo games on mobiles, for most of its history, you've only been able to play these experiences in one place. On a Nintendo console or Nintendo handheld.

In 2017, Nintendo shocked the world with its latest creation, the Nintendo Switch. This combined the concept of a console and a handheld into one device. It forgoes raw power for functionality, building a machine that's perfect for families at home or on the go. As a parent, your children have no doubt made you aware of just how awesome the Nintendo Switch is to play.

But is a Nintendo Switch right for your family? Do you need to get an additional hardware or subscriptions? And if you do get the Nintendo Switch, or you have one already, what are the best child-friendly games out there you should invest in?

As a parent of three young children who has worked as a video games journalist for over 20-years, these are the questions I'm frequently asked by other parents. The Nintendo Switch isn't a cheap investment, but it's one that can provide endless hours of joy for your children, an interactive entertainment experience that can get the whole family active together, and even provide some educational benefits.

In this book I'm going to provide you, a parent of young children who want a Nintendo Switch, all the information you need to invest your money wisely. The fun starts now.

What is the Nintendo Switch?

The Nintendo Switch launched on March 3, 2017. The price of the console varies greatly depending on your country, and as it has been out for three years, there are deals to be found. As such, I'm not going to put a price here. Needless to say, no matter where you are if you get a console, an extra controller or two and a couple games, you'll be making an investment of over $500.

The Nintendo Switch is unlike any other console released before. It's the smallest console ever made. In fact, it's not much bigger than an adult male's hand. But there is a reason for this. The Switch can switch play styles at any time. In fact, the console is almost like a tablet, with a touchscreen that goes down its full length and with motion-controls built inside. When you are at home, you can slide the Switch console into a dock and that connects it to your TV, as well as charge the battery. So, just like a normal console.

However, at any point you can slide the whole console out of the dock and switch (get it?) it to a handheld. It happens seamlessly and instantly, and the games look incredible on the smaller screen while playing in your hands. The battery hangs in there for about three to six hours depending on how recent the model is and what activities you play with it, too.

But this is not the only mode you can switch to. As well as Console Mode and Handheld Mode, there is also Tabletop Mode. This is when you detach the console from the dock and take it on the road. There is a kickstand in the back of it that will let you set down the screen and play like it is a mini-TV.

This is great if you bump into a friend in the playground or on holidays and want to have a quick splitscreen multiplayer session. But how is this all possible? Well, it's thanks to the Joy-Con controllers.

Introducing the Joy-Con controllers

We're used to Nintendo innovating with their controllers, and the company has done it again with the Switch. The Joy-Con controllers are strange looking things: there is a left one and a right one. They can be attached to the screen in Handheld Mode or attached to a small plastic device called a Grip in Console Mode, so it feels like a normal controller. Sliding them in and out of their little rails is a cinch and feels strong and well built, too.

You can also just hold them in your hands without attaching them to anything like a Wii-mote – only you don't have to point them at the screen. This means that in motion-based games, you can move the Joy-Cons any way you like through the air to perform actions in the game. It also means you can just have your hands relaxed by your side when you play; even if it is a big adventure game like Zelda.

It feels weird playing in this way. But you have all the sticks and buttons available, even if the left and right Joy-Cons aren't attached to the Grip peripheral.

There is another way you can play with the Joy-Con. You can hold them horizontally, where they become like old-school SNES controllers. This is particularly handy in Tabletop Mode as it turns one controller into two. This allows you to pass one to a friend so you can play multiplayer games like Mario Kart 8 Deluxe no matter where you are. Such a cool idea.

Oh, did we mention there is an infrared camera in the right Joy-Con as well that can measure distances and see shapes? For example, you can play paper, scissors, rock and the controller can tell which one you chose from the shape of your hand. The right Joy-Con also has an NFC sensor in it, which is used to connect with all your Amiibo figurines. This unlocks bonuses in plenty of games.

The Joy-Con is a little small in an adult's hands, it must be said. We'll touch on the Pro Controller later, but it's a good option for parents who want to play; especially if you're coming across from an Xbox or PlayStation experience.

What's in the Box?

When you buy the Nintendo Switch, there are two versions to choose from. They are identical except for the colour of the left and right Joy-Con controllers. In one version they are boring old grey for those boring old adults, and in the other the left is bright blue and the right bright red – totally the cooler version! You will also get the Switch Grip, which can hold the two Joy-Con halves together, so you have a more traditional controller to use. There is also the dock, some Switch Straps and the cables you need to get playing.

What's not in the Box?

Perhaps the biggest disappointment is that there is no game in the box unless you buy a model that comes in a pre-packaged deal. So, no Wii Sports or Nintendo Land or anything like that which we've seen in the past – you will have to buy a game to play when you get the console and we'll take you through the options shortly.

There is also no Pro Controller, so if you want to play with a similar controller to the Xbox One and PlayStation 4, you will need to buy that for extra.

Finally, the Switch Grip that comes in the box does not charge your Joy-Con controllers, it only holds them. There is a Grip you can buy that also charges, but we don't think that is necessary.

How does the Switch compare?

The Nintendo Switch isn't as powerful as the Xbox One or PlayStation 4, and there are a lot of big games that will come to those formats that may never come to the Switch. That is the only bad thing about this console though. Everything else is awesome.

The unique new controllers, fantastic ability to take the console with you wherever you go, and amazing library of Nintendo games are hard to beat. Especially if you love playing games with friends or are sick of not being able to play because someone is watching the TV. If that sounds like you, then totally get a Switch: you won't be disappointed.

What is the Nintendo Switch Lite?

Years after the initial release, Nintendo finally revealed a remodelled version of its Switch console, although it's not about something making faster and more powerful. Instead, this is just as powerful, but scaled down to be more of a handheld.

As a result, the Joy-Con controllers are attached to the side, it's a bit smaller, there is no kickstand on the back, and you can't dock it to your TV. But it does play pretty much all the same games, and it costs around $120 to $140 less than the main Switch console. So, it's definitely a good option if you want a handheld gaming device only.

WHERE TO BUY A SWITCH

Unlike a lot of consumer technology, video game consoles - and in particular Nintendo video game consoles - tend to hold their value. Just because it's been out for over three years doesn't mean you can expect to find that prices have been slashed over time.

You also won't find a huge difference between retailers. Shops don't tend to make much money on video game consoles, instead selling them at close to cost and then looking to make a margin on the games and - in particular - pre-owned titles.

Where you may be able to find some added value is in bundles, where the Nintendo Switch console is sold alongside some games. Or, as mentioned in the previous chapter, you can opt for the Nintendo Switch Lite, which is used as a handheld device exclusively.

Second-hand devices are obviously worth considering, especially if they come with a stack of games. There are a few things to consider. As time has passed, newer Nintendo Switch consoles have had internal improvements, especially to battery life. So, depending on the age of a console you buy you may be getting a weaker machine.

Also note that the Joy-Con controllers attached to the sides of the device do break or become unreliable if mistreated. Plus, as the whole Switch is more-or-less a screen, you have the same potential scratch and crack issues you would expect from a phone.

You'll find as good a price as any on Amazon, and you can hit the Buy Now link below to start browsing your options.

geni.us/SwitchConsole

Nintendo Switch Pro Controller

Like the Wii and the Wii U you don't have to spend hours playing games with the motion controls - you can get a Pro Controller. This is designed to be more like the controller you would see on other formats. The stick and button layout is different from the Wii U Pro Controller and more like the Xbox One – this is a change we like. The handles curve nicely into your palms, too, which makes the pad feel good. Plus, it has a D-Pad, which the Joy-Con does not. It's quite expensive, however, and perhaps unnecessary depending on the games you will be playing.

There are a host of knockoffs you can get on Amazon and eBay. Our experiences with these haven't been great. Syncing problems and poor battery life do seem to plague them. So, make sure you read a good overview of the reviews left on the various models and perhaps go for something midrange if you want to take this option.

geni.us/NintendoPro

Nintendo Switch Carry Case + Screen Protector

If you intend on taking your Switch out and about a lot, you should get a case for it. Nintendo has an official one available, which also includes a screen protector. Alternatively, there are cheaper Zelda and Mario themed Premium cases out there you can find. These don't come with a screen protector, but they do come with spots to store dozens of games and a cleaning cloth. Plus, they look cool! There are other companies making cases you can but online if you want something tougher or with more extras, so perhaps have a quick look on Google before you buy.

geni.us/CarryCase

Nintendo Switch Play & Charge Car Adapter

This simple little accessory could be the most important to buy alongside your Switch. As simple as it looks, it allows you to charge your Switch while in the car. It's built with a tangle free, flat cable and only costs between $10 and $20. So, if you are in the kind of family that is always doing big road trips to go on holidays or visit family, try and convince your mum and dad to buy one of these.

geni.us/SwitchCarCharger

Spare Joy-Con Controllers

The most likely thing to break with your Switch is the Joy-Con controllers. Not because they are flimsy, but because they get worked over a fair bit. Playing games, especially those with motion controls, and taking them on and off the console constantly eventually wear thin. So, if you need a new pair, or even if you want a second pair for multiplayer, they can be purchased separately.

There are a range of colour combos to choose from. I've kept the link below generic so you can choose the one that you prefer.

geni.us/Joy-Cons

Dock Set

If you've got a big family and multiple screens in your home where the Switch is likely to be used, a second docking station is worth considering. This is the base that the Switch sits in so that it can connect to a TV and charge. Without it, you can only play in handheld mode. Handheld mode works great, but I've found it's not so amazing on your kids' necks to be looking into their laps for hours on end. So, you can buy a second base station that allows you to easily dock the Switch in multiple rooms.

geni.us/SwitchDock

Joy-Con Grip

The alternative to the Pro Controller is the Grip. This is just a plastic device that allows you to dock the left and right Joy-Cons from the Switch to its sides. The result is a controller you can hold in your hands in a more traditional fashion. It's passable (especially for kids) and more cost-effective, but it's not as good as a proper controller.

Note, there is an enhanced Charge Grip version that does effectively the same thing, but doesn't just hold the Joy-Cons in a controller shape. It also charges them at the same time, which is pretty handy if you have multiple kids playing at the same time. Inevitably, someone's battery always runs out!

geni.us/NintendoGrip

geni.us/GripCharge (WITH CHARGER)

Nintendo Online Service

A whopping 18 months after the Nintendo Switch was released its Online Service joined the action. It had an immediate impact on the way you play.

On the PlayStation 4 and the Xbox One, if you want to play online you need to pay a subscription fee. Before the Nintendo Online Service went live, you were able to play online with the Nintendo Switch for free, but afterwards you needed to pay a subscription fee to get this functionality. So, games with big online feature like Super Smash Bros. Ultimate, Mario Kart 8 Deluxe and Splatoon 2 require the subscription to be played online.

Note: You can still play multiplayer offline without a subscription, which will likely be enough for most families with younger children.

The subscription costs aren't too expensive, less than $30 in most countries for a year. You can sign-up for it through the Nintendo eShop or the Nintendo website. You will need a credit card to pay. Note that if you have multiple kids, or you yourself, have their own Nintendo accounts and they want to play on the Switch under their names, you can get a family pass. This allows you to have eight accounts connected online.

As well as being able to play games online, the Online Service does offer other benefits. Your saved data will be recorded on the cloud, which means if your Switch gets lost or breaks, or you log-in on a friend's machine, you can still play your saved games. That's cool! You also get free access to a stack of retro Nintendo classics dated back to the 1980s and 1990s.

There is a phone app you can use, which links to various games giving you extra information and voice chat. You will also get special member offers and discounts. Nintendo Online isn't required and most families probably won't even use it unless you have older kids. But it's a small expense if you want to dive in.

WHAT ARE THE BEST GAMES ON SWITCH?

There are thousands of games available for the Nintendo Switch. The vast majority of these are indie games available through the eShop (rather than at retailers), but there's still a near endless supply of experiences to navigate through no matter where you shop.

Over the following pages I'm going to do some of the hard work for you. I've pulled out over 70 games from those available that I think are offer above average experiences for kids young and old. I've veered away from mature and restricted content in this guide. (So, don't get upset that I've left out your favourite shooter or hardcore RPG!)

I've also made an effort to provide you with some insights into the best type of audience for your family. Look for the key, similar to the one below, which provides some view to what you can expect from the gameplay experience.

Age Range = All, Middle or Older. (Older being around ten and over)

Local Multiplayer = Yes (Good for families with multiple kids)

Difficulty = Easy, Medium or Hard (with respect to kids' skill levels)

Genre = A broad summation of the kind of gameplay experience.

You can click the Buy It Now link to jump out and purchase a game that fits your need. Some games are only available as downloadable products through the Nintendo eShop. You access this on the console itself, so there is no link I can provide for those titles.

1-2-Switch

Age Range = All | **Local Multiplayer** = Yes
Difficulty = Easy | **Genre** = Party

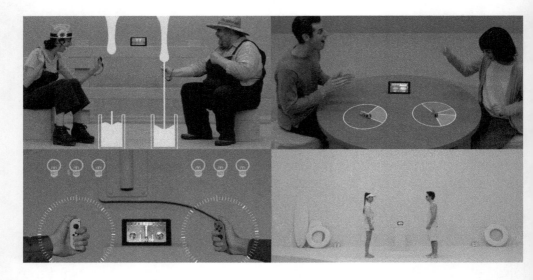

If you have the option of buying two games, this is what we would go for next. This is a collection of multiplayer minigames that is a bit like Wii Sports, but way sillier. They all make use of the Joy-Con controllers in fun ways to show what is possible. If you have friends or siblings over, it's easily the best game to play.

One game has you moving the controllers up and down as if you are milking a cow, to see who can get the most milk. Another has you pretending you are cowboys in a duel, trying to see who can shoot first. There's one where you point the camera at your mouth and open and close your mouth as fast as possible to eat food. And another where you need to try and catch a sword that the other player is swinging at you. Lots of fun.

geni.us/1-2

ADVENTURE TIME: PIRATES OF THE ENCHIRIDION

Age Range = Middle | **Local Multiplayer** = No
Difficulty = Easy | **Genre** = Adventure

The Land of Ooo has been cut off from the rest of the world. The ocean has flooded in, turning all the famous kingdoms from the hilarious TV show into their own little islands. Of course, this is the work of some evil dude, and our heroes need to take him out. So, to begin with, Finn, Jake, BMO and Marceline get themselves a boat and begin sailing the seas. They will need to find and reverse the work done by the Enchiridion, which has played a role in flooding the Land of Ooo.

It's a pretty cool idea for a story, right? It's not based on an episode from the show either, but is completely new and written just for the game. You get to play as Finn, Jake, BMO and Marceline through this adventure and make no mistake, this is a proper big adventure game. In the past we have seen the Adventure Time series switch and swap between all kinds of genres, but we don't think there has even been a game in the series as big as this.

For starters, it's a fully open world. Like the biggest adventures and RPGs, you are free to sail (in the water) and platform (on land) where you want and explore the various kingdoms. There are stacks of characters to meet and talk to as you go, lots of secret areas to discover and, of course, loot. Lots and lots of loot! You don't have to do just the story missions either, with lots of sidequests to dive into and enjoy.

As you might expect from a game like this, there is plenty of fun to be had just exploring and discovering all the areas you'll remember from the TV show. The visuals are really neat, capturing the cartoon-look so well you'll feel like you're playing one of the episodes. It's also awesome having the voices from the show as well as it really helps make this feel like a true Adventure Time experience.

It's not just about exploration, however, as this game has a lot of RPG elements. You will need to upgrade your heroes as you play, making sure they are improving so that you can take on increasingly harder bad guys.

Combat is turn-based and tactics heavy. As well as your normal attacks, there are items, spells and potions to manage, as well as unique hero abilities to unleash. Turn-based combat is not always for everyone as it's a bit slower than action-heavy games, but it remains a lot of fun here. Not only is it cool using all your resources to come up with the smartest tactic to win, the characters play just like you would expect. There are even lots of funny one-liners.

It's true, you never do know what to expect from an Adventure Time game and this one is a big surprise. It's a huge open world adventure with lots of RPG elements and plenty explore. Put on your pirate hat and walk the plank: it's time to dive in.

geni.us/adventuretimeTPOTE

Animal Crossing: New Horizons

Age Range = All | **Local Multiplayer** = Yes
Difficulty = Easy | **Genre** = Creation

A new Animal Crossing game is always good reason to cheer. They don't come out too often, but these epic create-your-own-world experiences can last you years. Don't let the cute characters fool you; this is a game of serious depth. One in which harmless entertainment whisks away imaginations and leaves gamers entranced for hours. Then days. Then weeks.

You start out with a tiny little patch of land, and by completing activities – fishing, farming, crafting and many more - meeting other characters and questing out into the surrounding world you can build out that patch of land into an awesome farm. And then even an entire town, all customised to your liking. None of these challenges are particularly had, but the chores will be reminiscent of those in the homes of many players.

This new game has you going one step further and taking ownership of an entire island. The idea is to build a thriving community on this island, and thanks to four-player local, or eight-player online co-op, many of the animals that come to visit will be human!

With a full time-of-day and weather system that literally follows the real-world calendar, there's always something to do and a new idea to explore in this epic sandbox adventure.

geni.us/animalcrossingswitch

ARISE: A SIMPLE STORY

Age Range = Older | **Local Multiplayer** = No
Difficulty = Easy | **Genre** = Platformer

One of the biggest new genres going around is the walking simulator. Where the act of just moving forward and exploring is the gameplay, with the world and music telling a story as you go. Arise: A Simple Story kind of falls into that category before going one step further with a cool time travelling concept. But let's start with the story.

You play as a wise old man from an ancient tribe who has just died and has landed in the afterlife. You journey through levels that have you exploring key memories from his life, starting at early childhood. While the story is interesting, it's perhaps too mature for younger kids. Which is shame, as the fun time controls really inspire young imaginations. They allow you to freeze the world, then fast-forward and rewind – sometimes whole seasons – to find safe passage. The platforming controls are a little loose, but it still can't stop this being a very memorable, quirky indie game.

ARMS

Age Range = Middle | **Local Multiplayer** = Yes
Difficulty = Medium | **Genre** = Fighter

This was a big release when it first came out! Nintendo doesn't do new series that often, but one rather awesome entry arrived in the shape of Arms. It's a boxing game with a difference. You hold the two Joy-Con controllers in your fists and throw punches for real to make your on-screen character unleash his attacks. It sounds simple, right, but it gets very deep, very quickly.

For starters, there is a huge cast of different characters and they each have different play styles and speeds, allowing you to find someone who is right for you. On top of that, there is a big range of different arm types that you can fit to your character, which offer various heavy and fast style impacts, as well as special charged up moves and weapon-based attacks.

Even better, you can combine them, and have different arms on your left and right sides, allowing you to mix up your strategy quite a lot as you discover new combinations.

The actual combat is deeper than just throwing punches, too. You need to rotate your way around the ring as you fight, throwing your arms out like you are firing a gun at your opponent. You can jump, grab, kick, deflect, block and combine all of these together at once. You can also put together devastating combos.

The motion controllers take a little getting used to, but whether you are throwing straight attacks, trying to curve your arms around objects or simply dodging, they ultimately work quite well.

Adding to the fun is the fact you can play with four people at once: so, you can team up with a friend and have two versus two battles, as well as classic one on one combat. There are other modes to test out as well and the whole game looks great, making this a definite winner.

geni.us/arms

BRAWLHALLA

Age Range = All | **Local Multiplayer** = Yes
Difficulty = Medium | **Genre** = Sandbox

Anybody who has played Super Smash Bros. Ultimate knows it's one of the best games of all time, but it does cost up to $80 to buy and that's before the DLC packs. Brawlhalla can't reach the heights of that stunning game, it's true, but it is free-to-play and still provides an excellent 2D fighting experience. It very much borrows from the gameplay of Super Smash Bros, with multiple players able to use power-ups and character-specific attacks to try and win a round.

You can play with up to eight people online, and there are over 50 characters available in the game with more coming all the time. However, for free, you will only be able to access eight of them, so that's the limitation. That's still enough for an awesome time and well worth the download!

Buy through Nintendo eShop

CRASH TEAM RACING NITRO-FUELED

Age Range = All | **Local Multiplayer** = Yes
Difficulty = Easy | **Genre** = Racing

Heroes love their kart racing, which is why it was no surprise to see Crash Bandicoot follow Sonic and Mario into the genre. This game is a remaster of the first of three Crash karting titles, released in 1999. For the most part it plays just as you would expect, with over 40 crazy tracks (including 12 battle arenas) filled with obstacles and power-ups.

Being a modern game, online multiplayer has been added, karts can now be customised, and the Adventure Mode has been ramped up with cutscenes and boss battles. There are 26 characters from the Crash universe to try out, too. So, while the game may not have the class of Mario or the team features of Sonic, it still delivers super fun tracks and four-player splitscreen.

DONKEY KONG COUNTRY: TROPICAL FREEZE

Age Range = Middle | **Local Multiplayer** = Yes
Difficulty = Hard | **Genre** = Platformer

We were so happy to see this brilliant game get a re-release on the Switch after debuting on the failed Wii U. This is a classic sidescrolling platformer, with secret areas, collectables, puzzles and lots of enemies to defeat. You primarily play as Donkey Kong, but can get a companion to join in with you that adds in an extra ability – Diddy, Dixie and Cranky Kong can all join in the fun. What we love about this game is the inventive level design. There are six islands to go through as you try and stop the Snowmads, an evil force that is freezing the tropical environments the Kongs call home, and each level has surprises and challenges that will blow your mind. It can get tough, but it's so much fun discovering what's next. Plus, the graphics are truly amazing and the controls perfect.

geni.us/donkeykong

Dr Kawashima's Brain Training

Age Range = Middle | **Local Multiplayer** = Yes
Difficulty = Medium | **Genre** = Puzzle

This "game" is all about improving the age of your brain by tackling minigames that involve school-like problems. Except, that it makes it all feel like a game, so you're playing, learning and improving at the same time. The series was a big hit on Nintendo handhelds, and the Switch version offers a similar experience – it even has you interacting with the screen using a stylus. But it also adds in new ideas, such as Joy-Con IR motion controls.

For example, there is a rock, paper, scissors game where you hold the Joy-Con, another where you count with motion controls, and another where you must pass the Joy-Con to a friend in remembering games. While not about action and adventure, this game is surprisingly fun.

geni.us/braintraining

Dragon Ball FighterZ

Age Range = Middle
Local Multiplayer = Yes
Difficulty = Medium
Genre = Fighter

Gamers are no strangers to the awesome Dragon Ball series, but this latest entry is quite different. It goes away from the huge arenas and big 3D fights we're used to, and instead goes to a more classic, side-on 2D view. The shift works a treat!

The full roster of characters remains, and their moves aren't overly complicated. It's true that this can make it hard to differentiate between fighters, but being able work out how to unleash huge combos quickly makes it a great multiplayer game. You can have up to three fighters on your side at once and tagging them in mid-combo is great fun. The action still looks spectacular, and the moves unbelievably over-the-top. Plus, you can collect special dragon balls during the fight, and if you get seven you earn a perk. Add a bit of a story to enjoy and this simplified Dragon Ball still kicks butt.

geni.us/DBZfighter

FIFA 20

Age Range = Middle | **Local Multiplayer** = Yes
Difficulty = Medium | **Genre** = Sport

When it comes to capturing the glitz and glamour of the world game, nothing quite matches EA's FIFA series. This is a game big on lifelike visuals and showcasing the most popular leagues and players. From the Ultimate Team to online play to managing and playing out a full season, there's not much this game doesn't have. Especially now EA Sports has added the Volta mode.

Volta is a new way to play based on street soccer. You customise the players, learn new tricks, visit street-based arenas all over the globe and play a host of different game types based on neighbourhood play. The intense five vs five (or less!) games are filled with tricks are a great new way to experience soccer. The gameplay itself remains quite a lot of fun. It's not as realistic or balanced as rival game PES 2020, but it's still addictive gaming. Especially against a friend!

geni.us/fifa20

FINAL FANTASY CRYSTAL CHRONICLES: REMASTERED

Age Range = All | **Local Multiplayer** = Yes
Difficulty = Medium | **Genre** = RPG

If you love your RPGs, then you know the Final Fantasy series. For three decades it has been wowing gamers and not just through its main series. This spin-off title came out on GameCube back in 2004 and brought with it co-op play.

A caravan is travelling through the world finding magic crystals and then giving them to towns so that can protect themselves from evil. Unlike the main games in the series, Crystal Chronicles takes an isometric view of the battlefield, offering real-time combat and puzzle-solving mixed in with cinematic story sequences. This much-needed remaster adds new visuals and audio, a more accessible multiplayer experience and even new boss battles and dungeons. It still looks old-school, but this remains a hidden gem within this epic series.

Buy through Nintendo eShop

FORTNITE

Age Range = Older | **Local Multiplayer** = No
Difficulty = Hard | **Genre** = Shooter

Unless you've been hiding behind your bed with your fingers in your ears (you wouldn't be the first parent to do that!) you will have heard of Fortnite. The online shooter is a cultural phenomenon and for good reason. It's a really well-made, fun experience. And while it does involve shooting, it's done with colour and flair and over-the-top silliness, rather than blood and guts.

A huge amount of the game is free, but your kids will nag you about spending money for cosmetic enhancements to their character (which are endless). They don't need it, however. There's more to just the shooting, too. There's a full tournament mode, big social community and a creative mode that allows kids to bring their imaginations to life.

It plays just fine on Switch, and given it's free-to-play, it's a hard to ignore. Just make sure you control how much time your kids play it!

geni.us/fortnitegame

GEAR.CLUB UNLIMITED 2

Age Range = Middle | **Local Multiplayer** = Yes
Difficulty = Medium | **Genre** = Racing

If you love your racing games and you have a Switch, no doubt you have Mario Kart. But if you are looking for something a bit more realistic, you should give this a go. In the campaign you do short races looking to get the results you need to up your level. You can then go into a detailed customisation garage, upgrading your car's look but also its abilities so you can go faster and turn better.

There's a range of assists you can turn on or off to make the game as hard or as easy as you like, but you get less rewards the easier it is. There is a rewind mode if you crash or go off the track anyway, so go hard! The game isn't amazing to look at when compared to similar games on other consoles, but it's not short on content. 50 cars from famous manufacturers, 250 races in four different environments and four-person splitscreen. The Switch doesn't have many realistic races, so Gear.Club Unlimited 2 is still worth a look from petrol heads.

geni.us/GCU2

GRID Autosport

Age Range = Middle | **Local Multiplayer** = Yes
Difficulty = Medium | **Genre** = Racing

For us old schoolers, the GRID series is fondly remembered by its old name. It used to be called the V8 Supercars series and in the early 2000s it was the best racing action you could get. During the PS3 and 360 era, the series changed its name to GRID and added made-up tracks, demolition derbies, gymkhana and even took away the cockpit view. It was still awesome fun, but we kind of missed the straight nose-to-tail racing of the V8 Supercars days.

GRID Autosport takes the series back to its raw racing roots. The cockpit view has even returned!

The three main pure racing styles are Closed-Top, Open-Wheel and Endurance. The latter forces you into a much longer race where you must think about tyre wear and make sure you don't overdo it as you race on into the night. The differences between the handling of the various cars, especially after damage and on different tracks, is really varied, which we love. GRID is awesome at making each car feel unique. It's also cool that you have a teammate and you can help each other out in races.

The two other styles of races are a bit more fun. There are Street Races, which occur on fake tracks set out on city streets – the tight corners and brutal walls make driving a real thrill. Then there is Tuner race, where you can tinker with your vehicle for time attacks, drifts and other challenges.

The career mode is pretty standard, but developer Codemasters has built on the excellent multiplayer. You can now form car clubs of up to 100 friends and all race for the same team. We really like GRID: Autosport. It looks amazing, plays well and the AI makes even single player feel like you're racing for your life. Get it.

Buy through Nintendo eShop

HUMAN FALL FLAT

Age Range = Middle | **Local Multiplayer** = Yes
Difficulty = Medium | **Genre** = Puzzle

Now that is a funny name for a game! You play this weird, fat little customisable character who is trying to solve some physics-based puzzles. Only thing is, he moves like a weird inflatable arm-waving tube man, so controlling him is super tough. Deliberately tough, like Octodad or Goat Simulator. As a result, he often fails at doing even simple things, falling flat on his face – usually from great heights – and otherwise hurting himself. It's super funny!

There are a range of environments, but they all have that strange clay look you can see in the screenshots. The puzzles themselves are fun to solve, but once you have worked out how to do them, getting your character to make the right actions without stuffing up can be quite challenging and frustrating. So, make sure you are in it mostly for the laughs and you are sure to have a lot of fun. Especially in the craziness of co-op!

geni.us/humanFF

HYRULE WARRIORS DEFINITIVE EDITION

Age Range = Middle | **Local Multiplayer** = Yes
Difficulty = Medium | **Genre** = Action

Hyrule Warriors was a surprise when it first came out, as it took the world of The Legend of Zelda and placed it into the brawling, combo-heavy combat of the Dynasty Warriors series. On a large battlefield, you need to defeat swarms of enemies so you can get to the generals that command the enemy. You then take them out to gain control of a portion of the map and then push on to the next area.

It is a successful mash of genres as it manages to still feel like a Zelda game, despite the over-the-top gameplay. The Definitive Edition includes all the extra DLC content, meaning there is 29 different characters to fight as and a lot of story to get through. We're stoked this game has come to Switch!

geni.us/hwde

Ice Age: Scrat's Nutty Adventure

Age Range = All | **Local Multiplayer** = No
Difficulty = Easy | **Genre** = Platformer

You remember Scat, don't you? He's the sabre-toothed squirrel that loves nothing more than his nut in the Ice Age movies. Each of the film's start with one of his hilarious adventures, as he gets beaten up by the prehistoric environment as he tries desperately to keep his meal to himself. It's some of the funniest animated action we've ever seen, so Scat absolutely deserves his own video game and guess what? He's got one.

Ice Age: Scat's Nutty Adventure is a classic 3D platforming adventure game. As you may have guessed, it's all about our hero Scat trying to get his teeth on his favourite nut. Unfortunately for him, it's locked away in a temple. The only way he can open the temple is to find four Crystal Nut relics scattered about the world and to bring them back to their rightful place.

The story unfolds through numerous cutscenes, each of which borrow the same energy and laughs that make Scat's moments in the films so much fun. As in, he gets flung about and smashed around. Sure, it's not the world's deepest game story, but if you love the Ice Age films, it's fun to see more of this kind of action. You'll even come across some familiar faces!

The game itself plays just as you might expect from a Ratchet & Clank or Super Mario 3D platforming game. You pilot Scat through the world collecting everything in sight, making your way through tricky environments, doing some light puzzle-solving and fighting off prehistoric beasts big and small.

There are ice chutes to skate down, river rapids to ride, tree canons to blast out of, lava to dodge and more, ensuring that things always feel fresh. It's also neat that some of the abilities you'd expect Scat to have – such as sneaking around, climbing up walls and even digging – are included in the gameplay.

Combat is relatively simple, but still plenty of fun. You can whip your tail around, unleash funny looking kung-fu kicks, fire nuts from a distance and do ground-pounds. There are also more powerful abilities to discover as you progress through the game that give you even more options. You can expect to face off against enemies like rats, bugs, wolves, raptors and piranhas, and there are boss fights to take on, of course.

We also must give a special nod of appreciation to the game's visuals and easy-to-master controls. Often with games based on movies aimed at younger players, we end up with experiences that feel quite underdone. But that is not the case here. It's quite a lot of fun moving around like Scat and seeing the world from his perspective. The ice age is a beautiful place to explore.

Perhaps it's because the game was developed by Just Add Water, a studio with lots of experience. This is the team behind the excellent Oddworld series and were a good choice to help turns Scat's film adventures into a nutty game. Sharpen your teeth and jump in!

geni.us/iceageSNA

JUMANJI: THE VIDEO GAME

Age Range = All | **Local Multiplayer** = Yes
Difficulty = Easy | **Genre** = Party

The Jumanji films are awesome. Filled with imagination, wonder, action and exotic locations, you don't have to watch them for long to know that it would make a good video game. It even stars The Rock, who is basically a real-life video game character!

As such, we were stoked to discover that the new Jumanji film, Jumanji: The Next Level, is being joined by a video game.

The game's story is relatively simple and is more inspired than Welcome to the Jungle film than its sequel. The world of Jumanji is in deep trouble and the only way you can save it is by locating precious jewels that have been scattered throughout the environment.

The first thing will notice about Jumanji: The Video Game is that it is not a 3D platformer. It's worth pointing that out as most video games based on family-friendly movies like to opt for this safe and fun genre. Instead, this game is a full-on action title with a massive focus on combat. Not only that, it wants you to play with friends. You can take it online or play splitscreen with up to three friends. How cool is that?

As such, the game pulls four key characters from the film and allows you to choose which hero you want to play. Dr. Bravestone, Ruby, Mouse and Prof. Shelley are on hand, and the art team has done a good job of making them look like the actors from the films. Imagine The Rock, Jack Black, Kevin Hart and Karen Gillan in a Fortnite visual style and you'll know what to expect.

Let's start with the combat, because it is so much fun and a big focus of the gameplay. Played from the third-person perspective, combat comes with a mix of brutal hand-to-hand moves, as well as long range gun-like attacks. As a co-op game, the idea is to approach the large fighting sections as a team, using each character's strength's intelligently, or even combing your abilities together.

The result is addictive gameplay as there is just so much going on. Plus, we like the way you're encouraged to give each level multiple turns. With each attempt you unlock not only new outfits, but also weapon styles, which gives you different strategies on how to approach a level run.

There's so much more going on in this game, too. Some areas have booby trap filled hallways and temples to get through, where spikes surge out of the ground and blades fizz through the air. Not only does it feel a lot like the movie set pieces in these moments, but you also feel like a proper treasure hunter making your way through ancient tombs and ruins.

Even the environments themselves look great, capturing that feeling of being in exotic jungle environments. You'll even come across animals like giant angry hippos and charging rhinos you will need to negotiate.

Opting for the co-operative action gaming experience was a great idea for Jumanji: The Video Game. Not only, like the characters in the film itself, is it better playing with others, but the sense that you can keep coming back for more fun round after round means you get a lot of bang for your buck. Now go find those jewels!

geni.us/jumanjigame

Kirby Star Allies

Age Range = All | **Local Multiplayer** = Yes
Difficulty = Easy | **Genre** = Platformer

The Kirby series always delivers great gameplay and it's no different on Switch. At first Star Allies may appear like other games in the series, with sidescrolling gameplay that has you avoiding obstacles, getting collectables and absorbing powers. However, there some key new features that really change the gameplay.

The most notable is that there are always four Kirby characters on screen at once. The game is designed to be played with friends in co-op, so if you are playing solo these extra characters are controlled by the computer. The best thing about having friends along for the ride is that two Kirby characters can combine their powers into new special attacks. In addition, Kirby can now throw hearts at enemies to turn them into allies. And when he has three allies, they can all team-up to do Friend Abilities. It's an interesting change to the gameplay that keeps it fresh and interesting.

geni.us/kirbystar

LEGEND OF ZELDA: BREATH OF THE WILD, THE

Age Range = Middle | **Local Multiplayer** = No
Difficulty = Medium | **Genre** = Adventure

This was the must-own game of the Nintendo Switch launch and even all these years later, it's still an unmissable experience. In fact, it's in many arguments for the best game of all time. It is, of course, the latest chapter in the long running action-adventure series The Legend of Zelda. It's not only beautiful, but brilliant.

For the first time ever in the series, you get to roam an open world, exploring wherever you want and entering dungeons as you see fit. There are new crafting mechanics and a great new climbing ability that lets you scale almost anything. You can ride around the world on a horse or drift huge distances with a hang glider.

There are some neat new special abilities, like the ability to freeze time, create ice blocks from water, throw remote detonated bombs and more. And it controls so wonderfully, with all of Nintendo's immaculate attention to detail in place.

There's way too much in this game to go through here. Not just from a perspective of the key characters and the journeys of Link, Princess Zelda and the evil Calamity Ganon. But just in the way Nintendo has made this world so real. From collecting resources for cooking food and magic potions, to tracking wild horses and taming them so you can ride them about the world, it's all just stunning.

The graphics, the story, the characters, the imagination – you'll play it for a year and still discover more. Just get it.

geni.us/TLOZeldaBOTW

LEGEND OF ZELDA: LINK'S AWAKENING, THE

Age Range = Middle | **Local Multiplayer** = No
Difficulty = Medium | **Genre** = Adventure

It's hard to believe this is a remake of a game that first appeared on the Game Boy in 1993. Yeah it has old-school, top-down RPG gameplay, but the visuals, controls and mechanics have all been redone. It looks, feels and plays just like a modern game, even if it's a different kind of Zelda game.

For starters, Princess Zelda doesn't play a role in this title and nor does the world of Hyrule. Instead our hero Link finds himself shipwrecked on a new island and must find eight musical instruments in order to awaken the local god, Whale Fish, so he can escape. While the setting is different, the puzzle-solving, exploration, dungeons and boss battles are as incredibly fun here as they always are.

geni.us/zeldaLA

44

LEGO CITY UNDERCOVER

Age Range = All | **Local Multiplayer** = Yes
Difficulty = Medium | **Genre** = Action

Originally released on the Wii U back in 2013, Lego City Undercover has been remade for the Nintendo Switch. This was great news, as despite being the most unusual Lego game released in the series, it's awesome. Instead of being based on a famous movie or comic, it's based off the actual Lego toys themselves. Namely, the Lego City range, although other themes like space also show up.

The story is completely new. It stars police officer Chase McCain. He has just been asked to return to Lego City after moving away because his old enemy Rex Fury has broken out of prison. Fury and his thugs have started a new crime wave, so Chase and his bumbling sidekick need to stop the bad dudes and regain control of the city. It a great story that is hilariously told. You'll love watching the cutscenes and meeting all the characters.

If an all new story wasn't exciting enough, there is also a big open world to roam. You can just about go anywhere and do anything.

Jumping into a car and just driving around is a stack of fun itself as there are lots of different regions in the city. Plus, there is a lot of detail and the improved visuals in this new HD version really make the city feel alive. Wait to see the damage you can do in a monster truck – it's so much fun bashing through objects in the world, and even watching your vehicle slowly disintegrate. There are other kinds of vehicles as well, including helicopters and boats.

There's plenty to do in the world. There's standard stuff like collecting things, entering challenges (like races) and doing little sidequests, but also weird stuff like finding lost pigs, busting thieves and capturing aliens. Then there are the missions. These feel more like the normal platforming levels we are used to from the other Lego games. As you progress you unlock new costumes and putting these on – and therefore going undercover – gives you special abilities you need to get past various obstacles in the world.

Elsewhere you will need to keep an eye out for rare super bricks you can collect, which you can then use to create the impressive super builds. These are a lot bigger than anything else you would have built before in the other Lego games, and include awesome stuff like spaceships and bridges.

The one big new addition to this re-release of the game is a co-op mode. It was always a big missing feature given how much co-op plays a role in this series. But now it is back, and it makes this great game double the fun.

geni.us/legocityUC

LEGO DC SUPER-VILLAINS

Age Range = All | **Local Multiplayer** = Yes
Difficulty = Easy | **Genre** = Adventure

What is a superhero without a super-villain? It may sound like a silly question to ask, but if all the villains were just normal criminals, then you'd just need normal police to take them out. But if you have a super-villain – an evil-doer with awesome powers, abilities and gadgets – then you need a superhero to take them down. Right?

That's what got us excited about this Lego game. It's the first time that a game in this legendary series has focused on the baddies. It's a spin-off from the three LEGO Batman games, and as you no doubt guessed, it stars all the characters the dark knight is usually fighting against.

It's got quite a cool story. As we've seen before in the world of comics, it all begins with an attempted prison break as bad guys like The Joker and Lex Luther try to cause havoc. Expecting to get taken down by the Justice League, the bad guys are surprised when a new group of superheroes turn up. They look like the usual heroes from the Justice League, but they are called the Justice Syndicate.

It turns out that the Justice Syndicate is made up of heroes from another universe, and at first it seems like they have appeared on Earth to help fight off the super-villains. But it turns out it's not the case. Instead, the Justice Syndicate plan on destroying the world. All of a sudden, the super-villains need to get together – as the Injustice League, of course – and fight back against these pretend heroes.

Wait? So, does that mean the bad guys become the good guys? Well you're going to have to play through the story to find out. But as we've come to expect from the LEGO games, the journey is filled with silly, over-the-top sequences that will make you laugh. There is a full voice-cast in action, so despite being a new story, it feels authentic.

By now you should have a good idea of how the games in this series play. While there are always fantastic new stories, abilities and ideas to try out in a new LEGO game, they all have the same core play style. You look down upon these obstacles filled worlds, platforming and fighting your way through waves of enemies. You collect lots of studs and solve puzzles by breaking things apart and rebuilding them. This is a LEGO world after all.

New to this game, and pretty awesome, is the ability to create your own hero. In fact, this hero is the main character in the story, so whoever you create will play a large role. How cool is it that you get to create your own DC super-villain and then actually watch them play in this world with other famous characters? It's such a great idea!

Of course, you can go through the whole game with a friend in co-op, which is our favourite way to play. You control dozens of different characters during the game as well, and even though you have your own villain, you will still swap between other characters. This could be to try out their unique moves or to help get past puzzles.

The developer has once again upped the scale of the visuals, and the amount of action that unfolds on screen is great. There is always so much going on, ensuring you're sucked into the game world right from the start. There may be a lot of LEGO games that come out each year, but it's hard to get tired of them when they are this much fun!

geni.us/legoDCSV

LEGO JURASSIC WORLD

Age Range = All | **Local Multiplayer** = Yes
Difficulty = Easy | **Genre** = Adventure

If you missed Lego Jurassic World when it first came out back in 2015, it's turned up on Switch with all the DLC included. We love all the Lego games, which provide laugh-out-loud funny, easy to play co-op adventure games to enjoy with your friends. The best titles are the ones that remake classic films, but poke fun at the most memorable scenes and the iconic characters. This game does exactly that to the first four Jurassic Park films.

It's true that if you have played some of the more recent Lego games this entry might feel a little unambitious, but despite the simpler gameplay, it's still fun. Solving puzzles through dismantling and building Lego objects, and battling enemies to watch them explode into bits, is as addictive as ever. Oh, did we mention you get to play as a Lego dinosaur?!

geni.us/JWLego

LEGO MARVEL SUPER HEROES 2

Age Range = All | **Local Multiplayer** = Yes
Difficulty = Easy | **Genre** = Adventure

If you're like us and you love your superheroes, this is the Lego game you've been waiting for! The first game in the series came out way back in 2013, so it was quite a wait for a sequel to finally land on the Switch. Thankfully it arrived jam-packed with a cool new story, a great new mode, and more superheroes than you can count.

The story involves bad dude Kang the Conqueror, who can time-travel, which should give you an early idea of where this tale is heading. It means that all the Marvel characters, no matter what era or reality they come from, can come into the story and help the fight back against Kang. They're all linked together through a big, new open-world area called Chronopolis. It turns out Kang has been kidnapping entire cities and relocating them to this place.

So, within Chronopolis there are 18 different Marvel locations, so there's plenty of variation. One minute you could be in Ancient Egypt or The Old West, then the next you are on Planet Hulk or New York City in 2099. Plus, as the superheroes work together to fight back, they begin learning some of Kang's technology.

This opens up more abilities and powers for our heroes. This includes time travel, which means you can age or de-age characters, changing their look quite a bit.

The gameplay is similar to what we know and love from other Lego games. There's platforming, puzzle solving, collecting and, of course, combat. Given that this is a superhero game, there is a bigger focus on combat than in other games from this series, with some pretty awesome action sequences.

There's one more thing: they've added a battle mode! Up to four players can select their favourite character and go up against each other. When you add in the co-op play during the main story, it makes this a particularly great game when friends are over!

geni.us/LegoMSH2

51

Lego Movie 2: The Game

Age Range = All | **Local Multiplayer** = Yes
Difficulty = Easy | **Genre** = Adventure

After the success of the first Lego Movie film and game, it should come as no surprise a Lego Movie sequel is not just turning up in cinemas, but also on consoles. As we've seen with past Lego games, this title doesn't just focus on the events of the new film, but also includes new experiences based on the first film and a few surprises.

For those catching up, in Lego Movie 2 an alien monster has turned up in Bricksburg and basically destroyed the place. To make matters worse, this alien also kidnapped a bunch of Emmet's friends and took off across the galaxy with them. Like the movie, this game therefore follows the story of Emmet, Lucy and their various heroic pals as they head out into space to kick alien butt and rescue everyone.

As we've come to expect from the series, while the story certainly resembles that of the movie, the developer has a lot of fun with it. Expect the already not-so-serious film to be taken even less seriously, and to laugh between missions and loads where cutscenes appear.

The gameplay, at its core, remains similar to all the other Lego games. Of course, this is a good thing as it works so well. You (and your friends in co-op), watch from an isometric view as the characters move about the levels, collecting studs, bashing up bad guys and solving puzzles (usually by building things). Switching between characters is easy and not only fun, but key to getting past these puzzles.

There seems to be a bigger focus on puzzles this time, as you need to come up with your own interesting way of solving them. In fact, a key part of the game has you locating rare items, materials and tools at your various stops across the galaxy. Building up your collections of these items will give you everything you need to solve the puzzle stopping you from getting deeper into space.

It must also be said that you won't just be on foot, with vehicles playing a role in the game, too. As this is more of an open-world experience, you can see why vehicles are handy. It's additions like this that keep this series constantly moving forward and fun. Discovering new locations and characters, and then working out how these new characters can change the way you play never gets boring.

If you're into the film, or Lego, or both, there is obviously good reason to grab this game. But it's also one of the best co-op experiences going around on any console. So even if you are not into those things (what's wrong with you?!), but want something to play with a mate, it's still worth considering.

geni.us/lego2

LEGO WORLDS

Age Range = All | **Local Multiplayer** = Yes
Difficulty = Medium | **Genre** = Sandbox

Lego Worlds is a totally different entry in the series to the other games you've read in this book. It's a sandbox creation game, inspired by Minecraft. You can think of it as Minecraft, made from Lego – doesn't that sound like fun?

When you begin the game, a random world is generated for you made from Lego blocks. That world is massive, varied and filled with tonnes of things to discover for those willing to explore. There are characters around that will give you quests to complete so you can unlock more stuff, plus there are creatures around to ride or fight.

If you don't like the way the world looks, you can spend lots of time remaking it how you like. There is a Landscape Tool, which allows you to remove bricks and rise, lower or flatten the land. There is a Paint Tool as well, which you can use to change the colour of bricks and to give them new properties – this allows you to do things like put sand somewhere silly.

Everything in the game is based around the various toy sets you can get in real life. There is a huge mix of toy sets and having them all available together in the one world can create some pretty fun and funny situations. It also means there are incredible number of items you can select and drop into the world. A lot of these are based on the exact instructions you will find in the real toys, but there are also some the developer has made brand new.

As you complete quests, explore, defeat enemies and change the world, you collect studs that can be used to spend on new items. This includes vehicles, which you can jump into and drive – or pilot – around your map. This makes getting around a lot easier (and fun!)

One of the most amazing things about Lego Worlds, is that you can build objects from scratch. You are free to put Lego bricks together in the same way you would in real life. Only, you have way more bricks to work with than you could ever fit in your home. Using the simple controls, you can place block after block, making unique and crazy things to show off to friends. Speaking of which, as well as two-player splitscreen, friends can also jump into your world through the internet.

The good news is, Lego Worlds is only just getting started. The Nintendo Switch version came with the first piece of DLC for free, which is the Classic Space Set. This allows you to go to the moon to build starships, space bases and deal with aliens. It has a real retro feel to it, and the space setting is a great departure from the rest of the landscapes and play sets.

More DLC packs followed, some of those for free, too. So, Switch owners got the best version of the game yet. If you like Minecraft, you better check it out!

geni.us/legoworlds

LEGO: The Incredibles

Age Range = All | **Local Multiplayer** = Yes
Difficulty = Easy | **Genre** = Adventure

Just how incredible is The Incredibles movie? And how much more fun was the sequel? It brings back the Parr family as they battle not just the Underminer, but also a new villain called the Screenslaver. The entire family returned - Bob, Helen, Violet, Dash and Jack-Jack. Plus, little baby Jack-Jack has some secret powers we didn't know about.

Now as you know, the Lego games love a good movie to use as inspiration. For the latest big release, developer Traveller's Tales is using both the original Incredibles movie and its sequel as the basis for its stories. So, you will get to enjoy familiar scenes, locations and characters as you play through each mission. Plus, there's plenty of laughs to be had as the story makes jokes about the films.

The game does have its own story to enjoy, however. As we've seen with other recent Lego games, there is a big hub world to explore here. Each neighbourhood in the world has been overtaken by a dangerous villain. As a team, the Incredibles family must beat all the challenges in an area, fight the big boss and complete the mission to try and clear out the world from evil.

By now you should have a very good idea of how the Lego games play. Either by yourself or – if you are lucky – with your friends, you make your way through a 3D platformer world, solving puzzles, building items, collecting bricks and using each characters' powers. Of course, switching between the characters and using their powers in different ways is key to success.

The first thing you will notice when you play this game is the graphics. Each game in the series has levelled-up its visuals, but we're still impressed by how much detail there is in the game world. It truly looks alive and filled with things to do. The activities you need to do in the missions, and the way that you use the characters' different powers, always feel so inventive.

For example, in one stage Violet creates a force field full of air so she can go underwater. While in another Elastigirl turns herself into a trampoline to help Mr. Incredible get to a high platform. The city, in particular, is a tonne of fun to just explore. Whether you drive around or use Dash's speed to run straight up the walls of a building, there's lots to see and experiment with.

We're always wondering which movie the Lego series is going to use in its next game, but with The Incredibles we were truly surprised. Despite the superpowers, this is not like the Lego Marvel games, but more an experienced focused on family teamwork... while beating up bad guys. Sounds good, right?

geni.us/incredibles

LONELY MOUNTAIN DOWNHILL

Age Range = Middle | **Local Multiplayer** = No
Difficulty = Hard | **Genre** = Racing

For a change of pace, how about tearing down gorgeous mountain sides from the seat of a push bike? The controls are simple enough once you get your head around when to tilt left and when to tilt right, but there is plenty of nuance required if you want to get every shortcut and nail the best times. The tracks wind through dangerous obstacles, cliffs and wildlife, making it challenging in all the right ways.

Your goal is to get down the mountain with the best time, and the risky shortcuts tease you into trying new routes. It's all physics-based, so the way your bike moves down the hill feels different each time, too. You will crash a lot, and often hilariously, but the game smartly puts you straight back in the seat a split-second later so the energy and "just one more try" nature of the experience isn't lost. If you like the Trials series, you'll love this. It's stacks of fun!

Buy through Nintendo eShop

LUIGI'S MANSION 3

Age Range = All | **Local Multiplayer** = Yes
Difficulty = Medium | **Genre** = Action

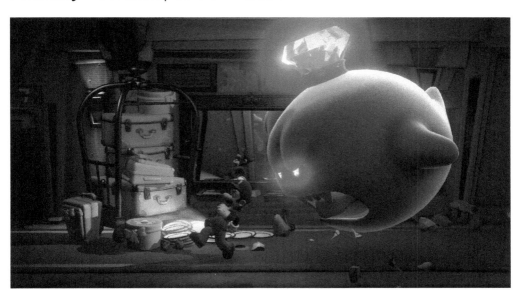

Luigi's Mansion is basically like Ghostbusters for the Mushroom Kingdom. Luigi and his friends book in to stay at a skyscraper hotel, but after arriving his mates go missing. It becomes clear that ghosts are involved, so Luigi must use his Poltergust G-00 ghost catcher to rid the hotel of spooks, while collecting coins and seeking out his friends.

What's really cool about this sequel is that each floor of the hotel has a different theme, which makes clearing an area and getting to the next very exciting. Also, the Poltergust G-00 has a stack of excellent new abilities, such as picking up ghosts and slamming them. We also like the inclusion of Gooigi, a replica of Luigi made of green goo who can walk on spikes, through bars and perform other ticks to help solve level puzzles. Best of all, these moments can be played in co-op with a friend. Alternatively, there are some party games to jump into with up to eight players as well.

Mario & Sonic at the Olympic Games 2020

Age Range = All | **Local Multiplayer** = Yes
Difficulty = Easy | **Genre** = Party/Sport

The Mario & Sonic Olympics games are great! The famous characters from the Mario and Sonic universes gather to compete across 21 sports. They can all be played in local or online multiplayer, too. Classics from previous years like Hurdles, 100m run, Boxing, Rugby Sevens, Gymnastics, Table Tennis, Archery, Soccer and Swimming are there. But there's also some great new additions, such as Surfing, Skateboarding, Climbing and Karate.

On top of that there are pretend "Dream" events, where you get pick-ups and abilities. Then there is a 2D retro mode featuring 10 sports from the 1964 Olympics. There are even minigames as well that play out like boss battles. That's a lot of great gaming!

geni.us/mariosonictokyo

MARIO + RABBIDS: KINGDOM BATTLE

Age Range = Older | **Local Multiplayer** = Yes
Difficulty = Hard | **Genre** = Strategy

It's one of the unlikeliest team-ups in gaming! The mighty Mario and the pesky Rabbids teamed-up in a brand-new turn-based RPG game. It's a surprising mishmash of different series, yet it's pretty amazing.

It's set in the Mushroom Kingdom, but this game is not made by Nintendo. Instead it is made by Rabbids creator Ubisoft, who are also famous for the Rayman series. This gives the famous Mario game world a slightly different vibe to what we have seen in the past, but it looks awesome. The levels really pop with colours and detail, helping to bring the adventure to life.

The story revolves around the Rabbids invading the Mushroom Kingdom and then tearing it apart. Why? Because that is what those silly Rabbids do! Mario, Luigi, Princess Peach, Yoshi and four heroic

Rabbids (dressed as the Nintendo heroes) team up to fight back against the invaders.

The gameplay is unlike anything you have tried before. You and your selected party of characters walk through the world like it is a 3D platformer, exploring and collecting. When you come across some enemies, it zooms out to a battlefield view. You then take turns moving your party members into position and defending or attacking the enemy.

There's plenty of strategy involved in using special moves and the environment correctly, but also linking together character actions.

There's one more extra bit of awesome for this Switch game that we have yet to mention and that is the co-op play. A friend can join in the fun with you on this adventure, and we totally recommend that they do. In fact, this game is so cool we hope Nintendo and Ubisoft team up again in the future!

geni.us/MarioRabbidsKB

Mario Kart 8 Deluxe

Age Range = All | **Local Multiplayer** = Yes
Difficulty = Easy | **Genre** = Racing

Mario Kart is one of the biggest game series in the world. Since the first game came out on the SNES way back in 1992, it has been one of the star releases of every Nintendo handheld and console. That's the case on the Switch, too.

Those of you who owned a Wii U may notice that the name of this Switch game is like the Mario Kart game that came out on the last console. Good spot! And you're right, this is not a true Mario Kart sequel, but is rather a hotted-up version of the last game from 2014. It includes that entire game, plus all the DLC, and then some extra special inclusions just for the Switch. All up it makes this the biggest Mario Kart game ever by a long way – it's huge.

If you didn't see it on the Wii U, the core Mario Kart gameplay remains the same as it always has. You need to choose a famous character and kart from the Mushroom Kingdom universe, and then race to be the first to the chequered flag. There are stacks of power-ups to pick up on your way, so you can bump and bash other players out of the way. Plus, there are boost pads, shortcuts and obstacles to deal with on the twisty tracks.

All the features of the previous games made it into Mario Kart 8, including hang-gliders, underwater sections and the ability to customise vehicles. New, however, is the anti-grav. During sections of the track that can twist upside down or go up walls, the bottom of the kart can stick to the track safe and sound. It's a great feature idea that makes the tracks some of the most spectacular yet.

There's also new power-ups to collect, including the Boomerang Flower, Piranha Plant, Super Horn, and the Crazy Eight, a huge power-up that gives you eight items to use. These can be used in the huge, 12-player online mode, too. Plus, there is also four-player splitscreen mode so you can play with your friends on your couch.

As you can tell, it was already a massive and awesome game. So, what is new? Well with all the DLC tracks included, there is now 48 in total to play, which is just epic. There are five new characters, which brings the total up to 41 as well. Two new power-ups are available in the Feather and Boo. And there are three new vehicle types, too. But these aren't even the best bits.

The coolest new feature in the Switch version is the return of Battle Mode, one of our favourites. This mode is not based on a circuit, but instead in an arena, where you and your friends need to battle it out using various power-ups, smart strategies and skilful driving. There are five different game types and we're stocked to have it back.

It's a pretty easy decision when it comes to Mario Kart 8 Deluxe. If you own a Switch, then you need this game. Get racing.

geni.us/mariokart8

64

MARIO TENNIS ACES

Age Range = All | **Local Multiplayer** = Yes
Difficulty = Easy | **Genre** = Sport

When he is not saving princesses from evil dinosaurs, Mario is quite the sportsman. One of his favourite past-times is tennis, and sure enough on Switch, he has run out on the court yet again. There are 16 Nintendo heroes to choose between, and while they don't vary too much from each other, they each have all the shots. This includes slices, lobs, top spins and smashes.

There are some great new features in this sequel, too. You can hold the Joy-Con and play with motion controls, even entering a quick pause so you can aim each shot before you swing. There is also now Zone Speed, which puts the game into slow-motion so you can reach far shots, and Zone Shot, which is so powerful it can break your opponent's racquet. In order to charge up the meter to unleash these abilities, you need to produce long rallies or pull off trick shots. These great ideas add even more strategy to the fun gameplay.

geni.us/mariotennisace

MINECRAFT

Age Range = All | **Local Multiplayer** = Yes
Difficulty = Medium | **Genre** = Sandbox

The mighty Minecraft may not have technically started the sandbox creation genre, but it's become the standard by which all others are measured. Don't let the basic, retro visuals fool you; this is advanced, open-ended gameplay that will get your imagination firing like few other games.

Dumped in a randomly generated world with nothing, your goal is simply to survive. By harvesting materials, you can craft items, which you can then use to build structures, hunt food and get the tools you need to be able to explore deeper into the environment. The game has been endlessly added to with free updates, ensuring the number of things you can do and achieve is limitless.

Plus, you can do it all with friends in co-op. A game that provides serious brain food and, quite frankly, is a must own experience.

geni.us/minecraftswitch

MINECRAFT DUNGEONS

Age Range = All | **Local Multiplayer** = Yes
Difficulty = Easy | **Genre** = Sport

It's the spin-off we never knew we wanted. Minecraft Dungeons shares the same visual style, creatures, characters and universe as the main creation game, but it plays like a dungeon crawler. A randomly generated, co-op dungeon crawler, no less.

The game begins with an epic cutscene about an Illager that is cast out by his fellow townsfolk and can't find a place to live. When he stumbles into a dungeon and finds the Orb of Dominance, it gives him the power to rule all the people of the land. He becomes quite evil, smashing up the villages of the people who wouldn't accept him and conjuring up monsters to do his nasty work.

And so it falls on you and up to three friends to go and do something about it. It's a classic "this world needs a hero" kind of story, and it's told with a lot of fun. In fact, it reminds us a lot of the Lego games with the silliness you see as the story unfolds.

You won't be crafting in this game, however, you do have an inventory. You will be finding lots of items in the world to either loot or use on the spot – such as food and potions. Each time you level-up, you are given a chance to upgrade one of your items, such as your armour or weapons, with enchantments that make them more powerful or provide magic abilities.

There are also artefacts you can discover that give you extra moves. These sit along the bottom of your screen like the loadout in Fortnite and work on cooldowns. The combat is simple really, but it that works in the game's favour. Linking your melee, ranged and artefact attacks together while dodge-rolling around the world is a lot of fun - especially with friends – and easy to master.

There's also a lot of excitement in just managing your inventory, discovering new loot and seeing what just unlocked enchantments do in the game.

The visuals take on the same pixelated look of the main Minecraft game, but it's not really retro; it's a pretend look. While blocky in design, the graphics are actually very polished and the lighting and depth in the world is impressive. There is a magical feel to everything that gives you a great sense of adventure.

The isometric view does have some problems. We did find ourselves getting stuck a few times behind trees or objects where you can't properly see your character. You kind of get used to this though.

Thankfully there is a big overworld to explore, from which you can select missions. These send you into levels where you need to complete goals, such as rescue Illagers. But you'll also find dungeons, which are randomly generated. These are particularly fun as you never know what to expect inside and there's epic loot to be found!

There's lots of games in this genre, from little indie gems like Bastian through to blockbusters such as Diablo, but Minecraft Dungeons still stands out. The co-op gameplay is great, and despite simple controls there is a lot of depth to be found. It also makes smart use of the existing universe, such as shooting sheep to get food, and it looks amazing. A must-own if you like Minecraft or not.

geni.us/MinecraftDungeons

MONOPOLY

Age Range = All | **Local Multiplayer** = Yes
Difficulty = Easy | **Genre** = Party

The classic board Monopoly has arrived on the Switch! The game is well suited to the console, where multiple players can sit around the screen and play together. You can shake the Joy-Con to roll the dice, too, and watch as your little monopoly piece makes its way around the board. The base game rules are the same, except there are five variations you can try out as well. There is also a Speed Die Mode for fast play – good for online! – and challenges you can take on.

What's awesome, however, is how the game boards come to life. There are different environments to choose from, with lots going on off the main board and in its centre. The animations for everything look so cool. Watching gaol bars drop down around you when you are sent to prison, or a new property appear when you buy something, is just so rewarding. And there is the bonus that at the end of the game, there isn't lots of cards and pieces to pack up! Hooray!

geni.us/monopolygame

Monster Boy and the Cursed Kingdom

Age Range = Middle | **Local Multiplayer** = No
Difficulty = Medium | **Genre** = Platformer

One of the coolest game series of the 1980s was Wonder Boy and this pseudo-sequel is inspired by those classic experiences. It's an open-world platformer, where you need to solve puzzles to get into new areas, explore for items, hearts and treasure, and defeat the evil creatures that get in your way using weapons and magic.

The developer has done a great job creating a cartoon-like feel, with great little cutscenes that tell the story, and bright, interesting levels. The best feature, however, is the animal transformations you unlock. There are six in total, turning our boy hero into an animal with unique powers handy for accessing new areas. Like a pig that sniff out hidden objects or a snake that can slither up steep surfaces. Old school fun.

geni.us/MBATCK

Monster Energy Supercross 3

Age Range = Middle | **Local Multiplayer** = Yes
Difficulty = Medium | **Genre** = Racing

Milestone is the best motorbike racing developer in the world and it's getting dirty again! This is the official recreation of the World Championship series. You can play through the entire season, with 100 riders and 15 stadiums across the 450SX and 250SX classes. You select your sponsor and pilot your way through the long career mode, but there is also online multiplayer and even a four-player co-op mode.

The real improvements, however, are in the graphics (especially the animations) and more importantly, the physics. Both on the track and in the air, racing feels a lot more realistic and weightier this time around. Hitting bumps and jumps has impact, while busting tricks is just so cool. Oh, did we mention there is a track editor, too!

geni.us/mes3

MONSTER HUNTER GENERATIONS ULTIMATE

Age Range = Older | **Local Multiplayer** = Yes
Difficulty = Hard | **Genre** = RPG

Games don't get any bigger than the Monster Hunter series. We know people who have spent more than 300-hours on just one Monster Hunter game! That's crazy, but it shows just how addictive and fun it can be to hunt down big monsters.

As you may have guessed, you play the role of a hunter, exploring a vast world with many different types of environments. There are four villages to visit, where you don't fight but instead trade, shop and talk to various characters to get tips on where to hunt.

Unlike other RPGs, you don't have a range of character types to choose from, instead it is the weapons you use and equipment you craft that grants you different abilities.

So, the way it works is this; you track a beast out in the wilds around the villages and defeat them in real-time combat. You can then loot materials from their bodies that you can join with other resources you find in the world to build even better weapons and equipment.

This allows you to track down even harder monsters, which in turn gives you even better materials again. So, you are always getting stronger and able to seek out bigger enemies. It's pretty cool, especially as you can also add special gems to your equipment to give them even more powers.

Combat occurs in real-time, but there's a lot more strategy involved that other games. There are 14 different weapon types, and each has four different play styles, so working out what will work against each beast is important. Especially as they can take a long time to take down – we've heard of some battles taking up to an hour!

Plus, this is no button basher; you need to play defensively and look for your opening.

This is a big game you really must commit to, but the controls work well, the graphics are great, and it can be incredibly rewarding. Our tip is to get a few friends together and take on the monsters in the awesome multiplayer co-op mode!

geni.us/monsterhunterGU

Moving Out

Age Range = All | **Local Multiplayer** = Yes
Difficulty = Medium | **Genre** = Party

Sometimes the simplest ideas are the best when it comes to co-op! Look at Overcooked, for example. Well this game has a similar vibe to that crazy cooking experience, except now you're a removalist. Your goal is to get into a place and get all the stuff out before the time limit runs out. Some things can be lifted on their own, but others require two people. That basic element of teamwork keeps the action fun, as well as funny. Sometimes you ended up trashing the place, breaking the windows and worse, trying to get everything out.

The levels get bigger and crazier as you go along, including full offices, farms and even haunted mansions where ghosts chase you about. You can have up to four players, and when you need to start crossing busy roads or rivers filled with crocodiles you start to get a feel for how crazy this game can get. Well worth a play!

geni.us/JSC5ZT

NARUTO SHIPPUDEN: ULTIMATE NINJA STORM 4

Age Range = Older | **Local Multiplayer** = Yes
Difficulty = Medium | **Genre** = Fighting

This is a 3D fighting game with a focus on over-the-top action. You battle in giant arenas where you can take to the sky or stay on the ground, or even battle on walls. Moves are easy to master and spectacular to unleash, causing huge amounts of damage to the environment, gear and weapons. It can all look a bit chaotic, but it makes sense when you're playing. The campaign's boss fights, and the multiplayer modes are where the most fun can be found.

Originally released in 2016 on PS4, UNS4 landed on the Switch in 2020 at the same time as the Road to Boruto DLC, so it's included for free. The DLC adds a whole new story mode based on the movie Boruto: Naruto the Movie, new characters and new fighting styles.

geni.us/narutoUNS4

New Super Lucky's Tale

Age Range = All | **Local Multiplayer** = No
Difficulty = Easy | **Genre** = Platformer

Lucky is a new generation of platforming hero. A cute little fox with a blue cape. Lucky starred in the 3D adventure game Super Lucky's Tale on Xbox One back in 2017, but it arrived on the Switch years later in "New" expanded form. The story sees our hero trying to help his sister protect the Book of Ages, which holds entire worlds and characters in its pages, from an evil cat called Jinx.

The game is broken into four big hub worlds, and then there are five specific stages that branch off from each hub to explore. In both the hubs and the levels, you can expect tonnes of collectables, as well as puzzles and combat. Lucky has some cool moves, too – we like the one where he can dig his way underground then suddenly pop up to surprise foes! For the Switch release, the hubs are bigger, there's much better controls, and you can expect more from the minigames, 2D sidescrolling levels and boss fights.

geni.us/superlucky

New Super Mario Bros. U Deluxe

Age Range = All | **Local Multiplayer** = Yes
Difficulty = Easy | **Genre** = Platformer

Yep, it's another forgotten Wii U gem given a new lease on life on the Switch. New Super Mario Bros. U looks sharp, beautiful and modern like any new game, but plays like the original sidescrolling games from the series' 1980's roots. Albeit with four-player co-op enabled and a heck of a lot more going on in each stage.

Levels are big and full of activity, using all of Nintendo's design skills to put you to the test. For its arrival on Switch, three new characters have been added: Nabbit, Toadette and (as a power-up of Toadette), Peachette. They add new moves that change up the gameplay nicely. As a bonus, you not only get all the levels from the original game, but also its sequel New Super Luigi Bros. That's a lot of great gameplay!

Nintendo Labo + VR Kit

Age Range = Middle | **Local Multiplayer** = No
Difficulty = Easy | **Genre** = Arcade

One of the big surprise releases over the Switch's lifetime was Nintendo Labo, which is part game and part toy. However, it's not like a Skylanders or a Lego Dimensions - it's more like arts and crafts. It all works with the Nintendo Switch console, and it's just another example of how imaginative Nintendo can be.

If you strip Nintendo Labo back, it is just a collection of minigames. In one you might be fishing, casting your rod and hoping a big fish grabs onto the bait so you can reel it back in. In another you might be on a motorbike, racing down a track. Or in a bowling alley trying to knock down the pins. Sometimes you may even be controlling a giant robot, playing a musical instrument or driving a remote-control car.

Each minigame is reasonably simple, but fun and well made. If they were part of a Mario Party game or 1-2-Switch, you'd enjoy playing them. But Nintendo Labo takes it all a step further.

When you buy the kit, it comes filled with cardboard shapes, mechanical parts and instructions. Much like during craft time at school, you then puzzle them altogether to build an actual object. Depending on which of the instructions you followed and what you've built, the pieces of cardboard will have slots on them for the Joy-Con controllers and possibly even the Switch screen itself.

You then use the object you have created as the controller while you play the minigame. So, you actually hold onto motorbike handles while racing, or a fishing rod while fishing, or put on a robot suit while stomping through a world breaking things to pieces. It works well and is definitely a very different way to play. Plus, there is a Toy-Con Garage mode that lets you mix and match, playing a racing game with the fishing rod, for example. How unique!

Finally, there is the VR experience. This is not the full, premium VR experience that we see with PSVR, but more like the VR we see with mobile phones. Like the other Nintendo Labo kits, it requires you to build the headset first from the cardboard-like materials supplied with the game. Depending on whether you get the base kit, or the full kit, you can then build other objects to use in the VR games that are supplied. The Blaster is in both kits, while the full kit also has a Camera, Bird, Wind Pedal and Elephant.

It's a neat idea and it's such a unique experience being able to build something and then use it in a game. While the games themselves are relatively basic minigame like experiences. Just understand it's not as immersive and mind-blowing as the full VR experience we see on PlayStation and PC.

geni.us/nintendolabo

OVERCOOKED 2

Age Range = Middle | **Local Multiplayer** = Yes
Difficulty = Medium | **Genre** = Party

Cooking makes for a surprisingly addictive puzzle game. You and up to three friends running a busy kitchen and trying not to crack under the pressure. There is always a lot of new orders coming in and food to be prepared and cooked. Not to mention dishes to be washed and food carried out to tables. Working as a team is critical to success and can produce heaps of laughs.

This sequel comes with a great story, too. The Onion King was reading from an evil book called the Necronomnomicon and has unleashed an army of undead bread: The Unbread! In order to save the day, you venture to some exotic, themed restaurants, working on new recipes (like sushi, cakes and burgers) and dealing with new disasters (like fires, collapsing floors and angry waiters). There are stacks of cool new ideas that spice up the gameplay, too. Like being able to throw ingredients, use portals and even drive vehicles around a world map.

geni.us/overcooked2

Pokemon Mystery Dungeon: Rescue Team DX

Age Range = All | **Local Multiplayer** = Yes
Difficulty = Easy | **Genre** = Dungeon Crawler

Originally released in 2006 as a Nintendo DS game, this spin-off series features all your favourite Pokémon as the stars. That's right; you play as the Pokémon. It's also less RPG and more dungeon crawler. You and the Pokémon in your party venture into randomised dungeons to complete jobs picked up from the hub town. These frequently involve rescuing other Pokémon, as the title suggests.

Gameplay retains the series' turn-based combat with a goal to levelling-up your team and progress the story. Like all remakes, it does feel a bit old-school; expect a top-down view and a more cartoony vibe. But new additions like mega evolutions and autosave help ensure new Pokémon fans will still find it fun.

geni.us/pokemonMDRT

POKÉMON SWORD & SHIELD

Age Range = All | **Local Multiplayer** = Yes
Difficulty = Medium | **Genre** = RPG

Every time a new Pokémon game releases it's a big deal. And this latest game – which comes in Sword or Shield forms, with slightly different Pokémon and gym leaders – is big in more ways than one. It's the first ever main Pokémon game to release on a console, giving us not only the best graphics ever, but a modern third-person feel.

The new region, called Galar, is based on England during the Industrial Revolution, and has a diverse mix of environments and cities to discover. When in main regions or wild areas, you walk around hunting Pokémon in the third-person view. But when you're on the larger overworld map, it's a top down view. Battling sticks to the random fight system, although there's new Dynamax and Gigantamax moves that can make your Pokémon huge so they can unleash different attacks. With new characters to meet, new Pokémon to capture and gyms to conquer, there's a tonne of gaming here.

geni.us/pokemonSS

POKKEN TOURNAMENT

Age Range = All | **Local Multiplayer** = Yes
Difficulty = Easy | **Genre** = Fighting

Those cute and cuddly Pokémon can get brutal when they need to!
This is a fighting game that mixes the Street Fighter 2D style, with
the ability to freely move around the arena like a Dragon Ball game.
Already available on Wii U, the Switch version adds in five more
Pokémon – Croagunka, Empoleona, Darkraia, Decidueye and Scizor – a
three versus three team mode, and online ranked play. There are also
32 assist Pokémon you can call into the action mid-battle to help you
out, although not directly control.

What is particularly good fun is the over-the-top combat, which
focuses more on action than tactics. As well as standard moves, there
are Special Moves and Mega Evolutions, which can be unleashed once
you have built up your Synergy Gauge. Fighting a friend is the way
to play and you can detach the Joy-Cons and play with one each for
gaming on the go.

geni.us/pokken

ROCKET LEAGUE

Age Range = All | **Local Multiplayer** = Yes
Difficulty = Medium | **Genre** = Party

As indie video games were just starting to find their way, it was surprise, instant classics like Rocket League that helped propel it into the limelight. The simple idea combines monster trucks and off-road vehicles with the basics of soccer. The result is a futuristic, high-octane, sports action game that you simply cannot stop playing. The field for these games is like an enclosed velodrome, with high walls you can drive up and trick off.

You play from the driver's seat of these vehicles as you work with your teammates to get the ball into the opposition's goal. While that experience in itself is endless fun, you also have a massive range of stunts you can pull off to better get around defenders and take shots. The strange physics and over-the-top visuals make it a real laugh and have propelled Rocket League into the conversation for most popular games of all time.

geni.us/rocketleague

SCRIBBLENAUTS SHOWDOWN

Age Range = Middle | **Local Multiplayer** = Yes
Difficulty = Medium | **Genre** = Puzzle

The mighty Scribblenauts is back and we are so excited. The series was revolutionary when it first came out, allowing you to write any word into the game and have that object suddenly appear. For example, if a tree was blocking your way, you could type in "axe," and one would appear so you could chop it down. Or "helicopter," so you could fly over it. The new Showdown entry takes that concept in a new direction: multiplayer.

Across 25 minigames, you face off against up to three other players in word-based battles, puzzle solving challenges and more. There are a range of categories, so there is a mix of game types to try out. Plus, there is a sandbox mode where you can just go in and muck around bringing weird things to life, as well as a campaign for solo players that involves a Mario Party-like board game setup. If you have never caught a Scribblenauts game before, we totally recommend it.

geni.us/scribblenauts

Snack World Dungeon Crawl - Gold, The

Age Range = Middle | **Local Multiplayer** = No
Difficulty = Medium | **Genre** = RPG

After years of success in Japan as a manga, anime and game, The Snack World series finally made it to the West via the Switch. Made by developer Level-5, the game is set in Tutti-Frutti where treasure hunters Chup and Mayonna (and friends you find) need to take down the evil Sultan Vinegar. This means fighting and looting your way through randomly generated dungeons, as well as a vast overworld.

Snacks are used to summon allies who will fight with you, which is especially handy against the epic bosses. An RPG at heart, you play from an isometric view, with the 3D world visuals and real-time combat all playing well. With plenty of characters to meet, towns to explore and a deep story, this is well worth a look.

geni.us/tswdc

SnipperClips Plus: Cut It Out Together

Age Range = All | **Local Multiplayer** = Yes
Difficulty = Medium | **Genre** = Puzzle

But this unique, four-player co-op puzzle game is great. As little characters in a simple 2D space, you have to solve a level by cutting pieces from each other to make shapes. This often combined with physics-based puzzles and various objects to make for challenging situations, even if they always make you laugh. It's just so cool trying to imagine new shapes and ideas with a friend in this game.

This Plus version of the game includes 40 new stages, two new worlds – one based on combi books, and another on a toy box – some new activities, new shapes to cut out and a new stamp mode. These additions bring a tonne of extra value to the game and ensure it is an essential purchase for people who own a Switch.

geni.us/SnipperClips

SONIC FORCES

Age Range = All | **Local Multiplayer** = Yes
Difficulty = Medium | **Genre** = Action

The fastest hedgehog returns with an epic adventure with fresh ideas. The story begins in a familiar way: Dr. Eggman and his robot army has taken over the world. However, he has had some help from a new villain: a mysterious evil being called Infinite. He needs help, so he recruits a team that includes the classic version of himself from a different dimension. This allows the gameplay to be a mix of classic 2D platforming levels and more action-orientated, third-person sections.

While this mix is cool, you can now also create your own character. You select from seven animal types, choose weapons and collect Wisps, which can also be upgraded and customised. Playing as your character provides a third gameplay experience, and in some levels, you can tag between them and Sonic, or even team up. The levels are quite awesome, too, filled with obstacles and action. Sonic is still a force to be reckoned with!

geni.us/SonFor

Sonic Mania Plus

Age Range = Middle | **Local Multiplayer** = Yes
Difficulty = Medium | **Genre** = Platformer

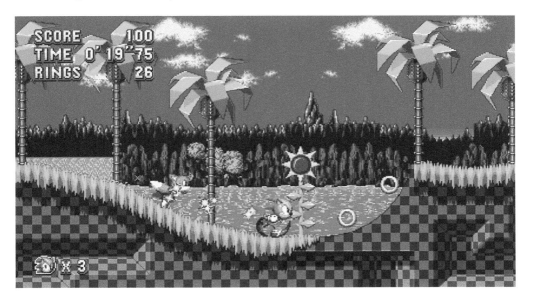

Sonic Mania blew us away. Staying true to Sonic's 1990s platforming roots, it was the best game in the series in years. It played quick, had great controls and unfolded in these massive, sprawling maps with lots of crazy traps and tricks to get past, as well as secrets to discover. There were bonus stages as well, that mixed up the action. Plus, the graphics, while retro-flavoured, were great. The details and animations in our hero and the various characters are easy to fall in love with.

Now a new version of the game, Sonic Mania Plus, is out and brings heap of extra content to the table. That includes two new characters with their own special abilities - Mighty the Armadillo (who does a ground pound) and Ray the Flying Squirrel (who can glide). There is also an Encore mode that changes up the levels, a four-player Battle mode, and extra cutscenes to enjoy with the story. Basically, a great game made even better.

geni.us/sonicmania

SPLATOON! 2

Age Range = Middle | **Local Multiplayer** = Yes
Difficulty = Medium | **Genre** = Shooter

Splatoon is a third-person shooter, except instead of bullets you fire coloured ink. And instead of being a human, you're an Inkling. These unique creatures look like boys and girls in their humanoid shape, but can change into a squid-like form at the press of a button. This is important during combat.

When you fire your team's coloured ink over a surface, you can swim through it as a squid. Not only does this refill your ink supplies (like ammo), but it allows you to move faster between locations.

Splatoon! 2 offers that same core gameplay experience, just a lot bigger and with a lot more action. There are a host of great new weapon types to enjoy – with more items dropping frequently online via DLC – as well as the ability to dodge roll and use a jetpack.

The online multiplayer Turf War game type from the first game returns, but there is also now a Splatfest mode, and a minigame like

Battle Dojo mode for two-players. More exciting is the new Salmon Run mode, where you and three friends team-up and try to survive wave after wave of enemies.

It's not just about multiplayer, and the solo Hero Mode is really quite awesome. There is a hub world to walk around, filled with places to explore and characters to meet. Then you can take off into these 3D platformer worlds, where you your Inkling's weapons and skills to get past obstacles and defeat enemies.

It's a big addition to the game and a lot of fun, tasking you with saving the Zapfish from the Octarian Army. This is another must own for Switch owners. Seriously, what can be bad about squirting ink everywhere? (As long as its virtual ink!)

geni.us/splatoon2

STARDEW VALLEY

Age Range = All | **Local Multiplayer** = Yes
Difficulty = Medium | **Genre** = Strategy

Boy has this simple looking retro game got depth. You play as a character that has inherited a farm from their grandpa, but when you get there you just find a little hut, a big mess and lots of weeds. It's up to you to clear some space, plants some crops, bring in some animals and manage your equipment. It's quite a lot of fun looking after your farm and selling off your goods at the local town. But going into town opens up another experience, as there are stacks of characters to meet that treat you in very different ways. They will also offer up tasks for you to do so you can earn extra money and equipment.

You can spend a lot of time just in these sections, but there's more. There are big mines that you can go into, filled with useful resources to find, but also monsters to battle. Managing your health and stamina underground while finding good loot is also great fun. All up, this is a big game that is tremendous fun and comes highly recommended.

STARLINK: BATTLE FOR ATLAS

Age Range = Middle | **Local Multiplayer** = Yes
Difficulty = Medium | **Genre** = Action

In this amazing game you play a space pilot in the distant Atlas star system. It's an open universe, so you can fly anywhere; even down to planet surfaces. You spend all your time in your ship, which is fully customisable. A chunk of the fun here comes from experimenting with different combinations of weapons and parts to create a unique ship.

The story sees you uniting the people from seven different planets to fight against an enemy using ancient technology to take over Atlas. So, you'll need to meet aliens and convince them to join your crew. The game supports splitscreen multiplayer, which is fantastic! The amazing graphics and gameplay aside, there are also real toy spaceships you can build and scan to bring into the game.

geni.us/starlinkBFA

Super Bomberman R

Age Range = All | **Local Multiplayer** = Yes
Difficulty = Medium | **Genre** = Arcade/Party

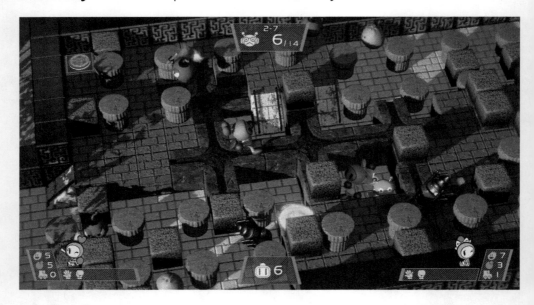

You'd think that any character whose main move is dropping bombs wouldn't last that long. Surely soon or later they'd drop one too close and boom, go up in a ball of fire and smoke. Yet the mighty Bomberman has survived for decades and is one of gaming's oldest heroes. The first game came out all the way back in 1983, and since then he has starred in over 65 games. How crazy is that. Despite that, Super Bomberman R is his first game since 2010, so it's been quite a little holiday for the bomb king.

Thankfully, the wait has been worth it. Bomberman sticks true to his roots in his new game. The visuals are all nice and new, the levels are bigger and better than ever, and the controls perfectly modern. But the gameplay remains very old school and that works well. The focus is on action, puzzles and quick reflexes – oh, and multiplayer.

Bomberman is a level-based game. Each level sees you looking from the top down on a maze made up of blocks. Armed with your bombs, you need to make your way through the maze, avoiding all the bad guys and obstacles, as well as collecting things. Sounds easy, right?

Obviously, a huge part of the game is dropping bombs as you go. This allows you to send flames shooting through the maze, and you must be smart about it. Flames can only shoot down open paths, so you need to not only time where you place them, so they get passing baddies, but also make sure you're not in the way.

There is a pretty fun story to follow in the main campaign. An evil guy called Emperor Buggler has captured five planets, using his henchman the Five Dastardly Bombers. Naturally, this is not very cool, so it's up to you – the White Bomber – and his many brothers and sisters to try and free the planets.

There are 65 stages to battle through in this story as well and the further you get into the game, the more complex the levels get. It starts with different types of enemies, which can move through the world in different ways and at different speeds, keeping you on your toes. Then you pick up different types of weapons, which can open new ways of progressing or getting past challenges. Then you get another layer on top of that as puzzles are added in, with little objectives you need to fulfil to clear the level.

Eventually the levels begin getting so big they can't be seen in one screen, with multiple areas to get through. It's awesome how the game just gets deeper and deeper the further you get. And that's if you play solo. What about multiplayer?

As well as playing story mode in co-op with a friend – which is very cool – there is a full Battle Mode. Eight people can play in it on the one console, or you can play with up to four people online. This mode is excellent fun. There are a lot of different bombers in this game you can play, each of which have different bomb types. So, when you're all dumped in a stage together, it's crazy rushing about trying to blow everyone up.

There's more to enjoy too, including the Grand Prix multiplayer mode that has you playing as a team. But by now you should know what we think of Super Bomberman R. It's stack of fun playing with bombs.

SUPER MARIO MAKER 2

Age Range = Middle | **Local Multiplayer** = Yes
Difficulty = Medium | **Genre** = Creation

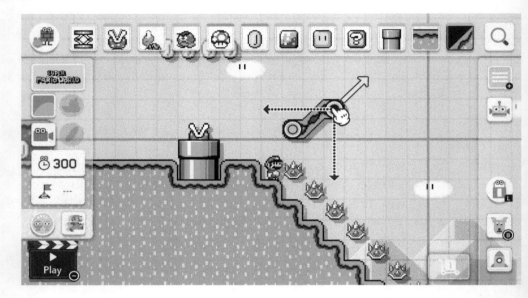

If you love getting creative in games like Fortnite or Minecraft, then this game is definitely for you. It's a level creator based on the 2D Super Mario games. The creation tools are simple to master and you're free to copy the traditional Super Mario style or create whole new styles of play. Think death runs, mazes and puzzles. Nintendo has added a tonne of new tools, as well. This includes slopes, vertical scrolling levels and auto-scrolling levels, as well as a tonne of new items, enemies, themes, vehicles and more. A lot of these are based on the 3D Super Mario games, like the Cat Suit, for example.

You can share any of your creations with your friends, of course, to see if they can beat your levels. We bet they can't! It's also worth noting that the game has received some sizeable free updates, including the ability to link up to 40 of your levels together across eight worlds. As in, to basically build a full Mario game of your own!

geni.us/SMM2

SUPER MARIO ODYSSEY

Age Range = All | **Local Multiplayer** = Yes
Difficulty = Medium | **Genre** = Adventure

Game releases don't get any more important than this. The biggest hero in gaming releasing a proper new entry in his revered series. This is not just the next big game in the Super Mario series, either. It's also the first open world Mario game since Super Mario Sunshine in 2002. So awesome!

What does that mean exactly? Well, rather than going through the game one level at a time, Mario finds himself in an open environment and you can do things in any order you like. This puts a lot more emphasis on exploration. It also means that his adventure needs to unfold in many more places than just the Mushroom Kingdom, and that's exactly what we get.

Predictably, Bowser has kidnapped Princess Peach and Mario needs to go and rescue her. He has a hat-shaped spaceship to help him out and he can use it to travel to different kingdoms. Once there, he must hunt down Power Moons, which can be earned by clearing various objectives. After getting enough Power Moons, Mario's spaceship can travel to the next kingdom. The range of kingdoms you get to visit is incredible, too. Some are like being on alien worlds, others like yummy fantasy food lands, and there is even one based on the real New York City here on Earth!

Of course, Mario has new powers as well. They mostly come from his hat, called Cappy. He can throw it out to hit enemies and can even take possession of their abilities. For example, he can use Cappy to take control of a tank, or a Bullet Bill, or even electricity! Plus, the cap can be thrown out over gaps to be used as a platform to reach new areas. It's a great addition!

There's so much more, too. There is a co-op mode! In addition, Mario can be upgraded and customised. And the game looks and plays as good as anything Nintendo has released before. Truly a must own.

geni.us/MarioOdy

SUPER MARIO PARTY

Age Range = All | **Local Multiplayer** = Yes
Difficulty = Easy | **Genre** = Party

Given this is the 11th Mario Party game, we're sure you've got a pretty good idea of how it plays. You and up to three friends take it in turns to roll dice and move around a map like a board game. Depending on where you land, you are rewarded, punished or entered into a minigame. A new Partner Mode has two teams of two freely moving over the map, working together to win. Plus, there's a Toad's Rec Room mode, where two Switch consoles can join together to create a bigger environment that goes across both screens.

On top of those great additions, for the first time ever there is online multiplayer, where you can compete in all the game's 80 minigames. Most of the minigames are good fun, either full of action, using the motion controls or laugh-out-loud funny. There are also a few super fun four-player co-op minigames. We only wish the game boards were bigger and more exciting!

geni.us/supermarioparty

Super Monkey Ball Banana Blitz HD

Age Range = All | **Local Multiplayer** = Yes
Difficulty = Medium | **Genre** = Party

Super Monkey AiAi isn't like most animals; he's stuck in a bubble. When an alien pirate king called Captain Crabuchin steals all the land's bananas, it's up to AiAi to roll his bubble through 100+ stages to get them all back. Each stage is set on a floating track and you must tilt the world to make AiAi roll. It takes precise control to keep him on the right path and not hitting obstacles or falling off to his doom.

As well as the main missions, there are also 10 brilliant party games to play with friends that challenge you to pull off hilarious tricks and stunts. It's true this game originally came out back on the Wii in 2006, but this remake not only features new graphics, but redone controls to ensure the game plays great.

geni.us/smbbbhd

Super Smash Bros. Ultimate

Age Range = Middle | **Local Multiplayer** = Yes
Difficulty = Medium | **Genre** = Fighting

Over 70 characters! Over 100 Stages! Does it get any bigger than that? And that's before you investigate the copious amounts of DLC content. This epic fighting game has all the modes you could wish for – including online tournaments and eight-player battles – blisteringly fast gameplay and stacks of new weapons, power-ups, moves, levels and characters to master. Plus, all the old characters and stages from have been revamped to bring them up to modern standards.

Gameplay is truly a wonder to behold, with the screen alive with activity and special moves as players experiment with a humungous arsenal of abilities. It's easy to pick up and play, but there is a tonne of depth, too. There's no better game to get you laughing all night!

geni.us/smashbrosult

TEAM SONIC RACING

Age Range = All | **Local Multiplayer** = Yes
Difficulty = Easy | **Genre** = Racing

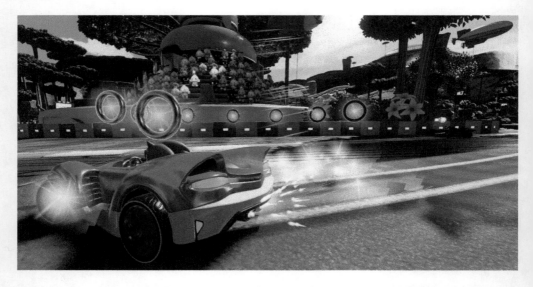

Jumping on the couch with three friends for a big karting session is always awesome fun! So, naturally a Sonic kart racing game is always worth getting excited about.

This isn't Sonic's first karting game, but this time he has offered a unique style of gameplay we have not seen before. As you may have guessed from its name, this isn't just about racing solo in the hunt for victory – although there is a solo mode if you want to play that way. Instead, Team Sonic Racing places you and two other players in a three-person team where you must help each other to beat three rival teams for victory.

Before we jump into the team talk, let's take a quick look at the core gameplay. Team Sonic Racing plays as you might expect at first. There are boost pads and jumps; and if you do a trick off a jump you get a bonus speed boost. There's drifting, of course. And stacks of power-ups, which come in the form of different coloured wisps. Plus, there are rings to collect that improve your speed.

There's an impressive range of power-ups to learn and master. Bombs you can throw, wisps you can shoot, one that makes you indestructible, another that covers up your opponent's screen, and more. The track design is excellent, too. With great, crisp and colourful visuals, the tracks really come alive. We love that there are branching paths, corkscrews, loop-the-loops and crossways to negotiate, not to mention various obstacles.

And of course, there are stacks of characters from the Sonic universe to choose from. They all have different car and diving stats, too, and these can be upgraded and improved as you play and earn credits.

The core racing is really a lot of fun. So, if you just want a great racing game to play on your own, you'll find plenty to do and a stack of different modes to try out. However, it's the main team mode that stands out.

During the Grand Prix events where you must race across several tracks in a row, the finishing position of each member of your team adds to your overall team score. The team who finishes the Grand Prix with the most points wins. As a result, working as a team in a race to try and make sure you all finish in a good place is a key part of a winning strategy.

Team Sonic Racing comes up with a few awesome ways of doing this. For example, the lead player in your team leaves a slipstream line on the track, and if other team members go in it, they get a speed boost. When you collect a power-up you can share it with your team and, in doing so, it increases its power. When you build up your Ultimate Meter, everyone in the team can press a button at the same time to get a huge boost.

Ideas like these – and there are more – mean that playing as a team really matters. So, you end up yelling out to each other, ramming other players together, swapping power-ups and more all in the heat of the battle. It works so well! There is so much in this game we haven't mentioned yet, too: like online play and four-person splitscreen multiplayer. A solid entry into the karting genre.

geni.us/sonicracing

TETRIS99

Age Range = All | **Local Multiplayer** = Yes
Difficulty = Medium | **Genre** = Party

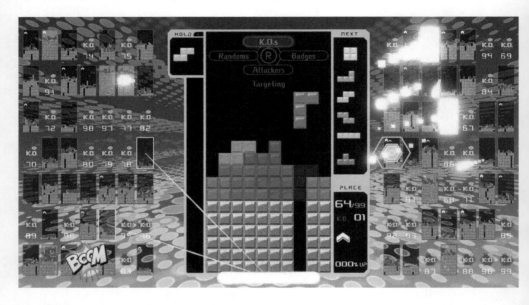

Tetris is a game that needs no introduction, but you'll probably be surprised that decades after you first played it on a Game Boy, it's still giving great entertainment to gamers. Tetris99 takes the battle royale genre and applies it to the falling pieces, puzzle gameplay everybody knows and loves.

As the name suggests, 99 players enter the same match online and begin trying to clear lines. As you clear lines, they are randomly applied to other players in the match, making their life much harder.

It makes for frantic fun and plenty of laughter, even if it can get quite tense as players are wiped out and your march to number one continues. Thankfully, if you have a Nintendo Switch Online service, you can download the main Tetris99 online mode for free, too.

geni.us/tetris99

TRIALS RISING

Age Range = Older | **Local Multiplayer** = Yes
Difficulty = Hard | **Genre** = Platformer

Trials is easily one of our favourite game series. It's effectively a platformer where you need to get to the end of the level as fast as possible. However, you are on the back of motorbike. Making it over the various obstacles while adjusting your speed and your braking perfectly is tough, but so much fun.

This entry takes us to real-world locations such as Mt Everest, the pyramids and the Eiffel Tower. We also get a co-op mode called Tandem, where two players are on one bike at the same time, which adds to the chaos. Elsewhere the four-player option remains, the trick system and the rider and bike customisation.

You can also build your own tracks to share with your friends all around the world. You can never play too much of the Trials series and if you like bikes, we highly recommend it.

TRINE 4

Age Range = Middle | **Local Multiplayer** = Yes
Difficulty = Medium | **Genre** = Puzzle-Platformer

Prince Selius has a problem. He is having horrible nightmares and, even worse, they are coming to life and threatening to destroy his kingdom. That simply will not do! Therefore, the Prince has called on four heroes - Amadeus the Wizard, Pontius the Knight and Zoya the Thief – to come to his aid. That is where you and your three friends come in; setting off on an adventure across the land that will require plenty of brain power if you want to succeed.

While Trine 4 is a co-op gaming experience best played with friends, you can of course play solo, switching between each character as required. Either way, the core gameplay remains the same. You need to use the different skills of the three heroes to solve your way through the world.

At first the puzzles are obvious, but as you unlock new abilities and experiment with the world's physics, you need to start being inventive with your solutions. Many challenges have multiple ways in which they can be passed, you see. There is so much fun to be had in finding a way to solve a puzzle; especially when you do it as a team.

Learning and unlocking the abilities of each character is where your skills will be most tested. As the wizard, for example, you can use magic to create boxes and then lift them through the air. This can help you move another player across the map, or to climb up to a high area, or even add a weight to something so it falls over.

The Knight can use his shield to reflect light, bouncing it around the world, or to bash through objects. The thief can fire ice arrows into moving objects to freeze them and attach robes between objects to create tightrope bridges.

This is just the start, of course, and you can imagine how the gameplay gets deeper as you level-up the characters and get new abilities. Controls are tight, with your classic platforming filling up the moments between the puzzles. There is combat as well, including boss battles. Even the combat uses the characters' abilities in smart ways. For example, the wizard can create one of his boxes and drop it on a creature's head.

It doesn't hurt that Trine 4 is truly gorgeous. This is what they call a 2.5D platformer, where you're sidescrolling across the screen, but the environment and creatures still have a 3D feel to them. Some of the environments are truly magical, filled with amazing amounts of detail. Even the voice acting is great.

There's nothing better than playing with your friends, and if you're looking for a great game to enjoy over a wet weekend, then Trine 4 is just the kind of magic you're after.

geni.us/trine4

UNTITLED GOOSE GAME

Age Range = Middle | **Local Multiplayer** = No
Difficulty = Easy | **Genre** = Party

Have you been wondering what this Untitled Goose Game that keeps winning awards is all about? It wasn't a big release when it came out in late 2019; in fact, it didn't even get a proper name. But since then, word-of-mouth has helped make this one of the most popular indie games going around.

It's a stealth-puzzle game, played from an isometric view as you make your way from one area to the next clearing objectives. The thing is, you're a goose. You move like a goose, and all your moves are goose-like. You can honk, duck, run, flap your wings and manipulate objects with your beak. You're often required to steal objects or trick humans in the village, and these puzzles play out in such a bizarre way it's not only super fun, but funny, too. The simple visuals and story only add to the charm, too.

Buy through Nintendo eShop

V-Rally 4

Age Range = Older | **Local Multiplayer** = Yes
Difficulty = Medium | **Genre** = Racing

We love rally games! Sliding around on the dirt and dodging trees at crazy fast speeds is an exhilarating experience. The V-Rally series goes right back to 1997 and it was always known for being an arcade experience. As in, easier to control and not so focused on perfection. This surprise sequel is more of a simulation, meaning it's trying to be tough and challenging. Sometimes it does not get it right and the controls feel a bit off or your AI opponents drive a bit silly.

The Career Mode is a bit lame, too. But there are multiple modes, including your classic rallies, rallycrosses and hillclimbs, as well as a few vehicle categories to try out, including buggies. There is even a gymkhana mode, which is all about drifting, nailing speed traps, precise driving and just being a total showman. The track design is solid, and the visuals are very sharp as well. So, while this isn't as good as the Dirt series, it's still fun and, most importantly, it's on Switch.

geni.us/vrally4

WONDERFUL 101:
REMASTERED, THE

Age Range = Older | **Local Multiplayer** = Yes
Difficulty = Hard | **Genre** = Action

Played from an isometric view, The Wonderful 101 is a bit like a Power Rangers TV show with its over-the-top enemies and insane action. But it's also super unique. You control a team of earth defence superheroes who rescue people from evil invaders. They then follow you as a big group that can morph into objects you can use. Think ladders, bridges, hang-gliders, weapons and more. Weird, right?

The gameplay moves at a relentless pace keeping you busy bashing up never-ending swarms of bad dudes. In fact, the game's biggest flaw is that there is so much going on it can be hard to see where you are, which is a problem given the difficulty. Thankfully the equally silly and funny story helps you forget these troubles.

geni.us/Wonderful101

XENOBLADE CHRONICLES 2

Age Range = Older | **Local Multiplayer** = No
Difficulty = Medium | **Genre** = RPG

There's no shortage of RPGs on Switch, but this could be the purest of the lot. When we say pure, we mean that it delves so deep into the role-playing element of the genre – like character progression and improving your weapons and gear - that it's a bigger focus than the story or the combat. It's certainly fun going so deep on building a character and even managing an entire army as you get deeper into the game.

The amazing world, which involves several continents that sit on the back of giant flying monster, is also awesome to explore. We feel that a little bit more could have been done to make the story exciting, as your journey to get to the World Tree is simple. And the combat, which involves timing your attacks and linking together combos, doesn't change too much as you go. But overall, this is still an impressive and huge RPG that will take you tens of hours to finish.

geni.us/xenochron2

YOKU'S ISLAND EXPRESS

Age Range = Middle | **Local Multiplayer** = No
Difficulty = Medium | **Genre** = Platformer

This is one of the coolest and most innovative sidescrolling platformers we've ever played. You play a dung beetle – yes, dung! – who decides he wants to become the new postman on a whacky island filled with all kinds of bizarre creatures. When he gets there, however, he finds out a mystical beast is attacking the local spirits and unsettling nature, resulting in storms, snow, droughts and more. This makes it hard to deliver the mail, so you need to stop this evil force.

Other than the quirky characters and awesome graphics, what we love about this game is the level design. Yoku is attached to a ball, so he can be hit around the world by paddles. So, you can move like a normal platformer, but the fun comes in treating the hero like a pinball and whacking him through this maze of passageways and bumpers. It works wonderfully, and there's always somewhere new to explore once you have the right ability. We love this game; get it!

geni.us/yokuislexp

YOOKA-LAYLEE

Age Range = All | **Local Multiplayer** = Yes
Difficulty = Medium | **Genre** = Adventure

They don't make many 3D adventure platformers anymore. Back in the late 1990s and early 2000s this was the most popular genre in gaming. Donkey Kong, Mario, Ty the Tasmanian Tiger, Spyro the Dragon, Ratchet and Clank, Jak and Daxter, and Crash Bandicoot are just some of the big names we used to love playing in big, open 3D worlds. One of the best though, was Banjo-Kazooie, which released in 1998 on the N64, and its sequel Banjo-Tooie, which came out two years later.

Can you imagine what it would be like if the same team that made the Banjo-Kazooie series all those years ago got back together and made a new game? And can you imagine if that game tried to be like a Banjo-Kazooie 3, with the same sense of humour and gameplay, but with awesome new visuals? Well that's exactly what has happened. And the game is called Yooka-Laylee.

The new characters – yes, their names are Yooka and Laylee – are a chameleon and a bat.

Despite there being two of them, you control them like they are one character. The various attacking and exploration moves involve the duo working as a team and they look great in everything they do. Our heroes have a big task in front of them: they need to stop the evil Dr. Quack and Capital B from stealing all the world's books. To do this you need to explore through five worlds, finding all the lost Pagies and returning them to the great tomes.

It's a typically silly and over-the-top story, but we love it. The characters are just so funny and over-the-top – in fact, often just completely weird – that we love talking with and battling against them. A warning, though. The story is all told in text, not voice acting, which is a bit old school. So, you will want to be a good reader to get the most out of this game.

The camera takes a little bit of getting used to as well, but once you get the hang of it, the gameplay is so much fun.

As well as the little home area you start in and the halls of your enemies' evil lair you get to explore, the five worlds are massive. Each has a different theme and is jammed with things to do and find. There are puzzles to solve, hard-to-reach places to get to, stacks of minigames (like races through the levels and arcade machines), quests to pick-up and tonnes of collectables.

We love how the game just keeps getting bigger the more you collect, too. Not only do we mean physically bigger, but as you unlock new moves and level-up your skills, you realise you can get to areas you couldn't before. For example, one of our favourites "moves" is the fart bubble, that lets you breathe underwater – too funny! The game isn't that big on combat, although there are lots of creatures to fight, and more focused on that exploration. The level design and awesome visuals make that very rewarding.

As a little bonus, you can unlock minigames that allow you to play multiplayer with up to three friends, too. It just helps make Yooka-Laylee a must-own. It's one of the best platform adventure games we've played in the last 20-years, and let's hope it helps the genre come back bigger and stronger than ever.

geni.us/YookaLaylee

YOSHI'S CRAFTED ISLAND

Age Range = All | **Local Multiplayer** = Yes
Difficulty = Easy | **Genre** = Platformer

It's always exciting when Nintendo releases a new platformer! Yoshi is the little green dinosaur that loves throwing eggs and using his powerful tongue as a weapon. His new Switch adventure adds more fun to the same gameplay we know and love. This time the story revolves around an artefact called the Sundream Stone that sits on the highest mountain in the land. This powerful device can make anyone's dreams come true, so naturally bad dudes Kamek and Baby Bowser want to steal it. Naughty, naughty!

As we've come to expect from Nintendo, it's the inventive level design that makes this game stand out. There is a new feature where the world flips around whenever you do a ground pound. So suddenly the background becomes the foreground. It plays into a lot of neat puzzles. It's also great that there is a two-player mode, giving you and a friend a chance to play at same time. Go Yoshi!

geni.us/yoshiCl

CHEATS

Animal Crossing: New Horizons

How to unlock Golden Tools.

- **Golden Axe:** Break 100 of any axe type
- **Golden Net:** Donate all bugs to the museum
- **Golden Rod:** Donate all fish to the museum
- **Golden Shovel:** Rescue Gulliver 30 times
- **Golden Slingshot:** Shoot down lots of balloons
- **Golden Watering Can:** Get a 5-star Island Evaluation

How to unlock new locations?

Able Sisters: First you need to buy clothing from Mabel at Nook's Cranny in excess of 5,000 bells. Then to unlock you need to talk to her the third time she comes to town.

Museum: Collect 15 different fish, bugs or fossil specimens. Then, donate them all to Blathers when he is in your town.

Nook's Cranny: First you must do your first house upgrade. Once that is complete, collect 30 pieces of wood, hardwood, softwood and iron nuggets. Take these to Timmy and give them to him to unlock.

Resident Services Building: This upgrade will come as soon as the first three villagers arrive that you have built homes for.

BoxBoy! + BoxGirl!

A Secret Ending.

There are two endings to this game, but you only get the real ending if you collect all four fragments of a costume first and wear them. When you have collected all four, make sure you are in the main A Tale For One campaign mode, equip all four and then complete stage 16-8. This will show you the true ending. This is how you get the fragments:

- **Fragment of Affection (Mouth):** Collect all crowns and box medals in "A Tale For Two"

- **Fragment of Bonds (Eyes):** Collect all crowns and box medals in "A Tale For Two"

- **Fragment of Courage (Head):** Collect all crowns and box medals in "A Tale For One"

- **Fragment of Wishes (Body):** Collect all crowns and box medals in "A Tall Tale"

Donkey Kong Country: Tropical Freeze

Unlockables

- **New Stages:** Collect the KONG letters on every level of an island.

- **Hard Mode:** Complete the three stages on the 7th island.

- **Island 7 Secret Seclusion:** Complete the special K level on each island.

Get a Kong Buddy without paying.

There's a trick to playing the game solo as a side character. Before you start a level at the World Menu, add a second player by pressing start on a second controller. Then Press A, select a controller option and a character. Once you're in the level, remove the second controller from the Add/Drop menu so you can play solo, and watch as the Kong Buddy character stays in the game.

Dragon Ball FighterZ

How to unlock extra characters.

Once these characters are unlocked you will be able to use them during the Story Mode.

- **Android #21:** Finish the game
- **Goku (SSGSS):** Reach Level 40 with Goku (Super Saiyan)
- **Vegeta (SSGSS):** Reach Level 40 with Vegeta (Super Saiyan)
- **SSB Goku:** Earn 500,000 zeni or complete the Hyperbolic Time Chamber Course (Hard) in Arcade Mode with at least an A rank
- **SSB Vegeta:** Earn 300,000 zeni or complete the Extreme Gravity Spaceship Course (Hard) in Arcade mode with at least an A rank

Play as different characters.

When you are at the V.S. screen, holding down the Left Trigger will activate your second character, and holding down the Left Bumper your third character.

Dragon Quest Builders

In the Terra Incognita mode, you can craft additional items after they have been unlocked. This is how you unlock them:

- **Display Stands:** Chapter 1 – Defeat the three dragons.
- **Builder's Workbench and Machinist's Workbench:** Chapter Final – Build your base to level 4.
- **Costume Set:** Chapter 1 – Build a Cantlin Garden.
- **Erdrick's Legendary Items and Gear:** Chapter Final – Collect 200 different types of items.
- **Featherwear Footfall Accessory (No Fall Damage):** Chapter 1 – Repair the hammerhood's graveyard.

- **Flame Blade:** Chapter 1 – Collect 150 different types of items.

- **Forbidden Furniture:** Chapter 3 – Defeat all the boss trolls and gigantes.

- **Forbidden Gear:** Chapter Final – Find the sword of ruin.

- **Gourmand's Girdle Accessory (Hunger stops):** Chapter 2 – Collect 200 different types of items.

- **Hot Water Crystal:** Chapter 3 – Complete the spectacular spa blueprint.

- **Lyres of Slime Immemorial:** Chapter 3 – Discover the recipe for the lyre of slime immemorial.

- **Meteorite Bracer Accessory (Run Faster):** Chapter 2 – Complete all of Thalamus's puzzles.

- **Novelty Items:** Chapter Final – Show a verdant vision to a certain someone.

- **Ring of Criticality Accessory:** Chapter Final – Defeat the Dragonlord without wearing the legendary armour.

- **Roofing Tiles set:** Chapter 2 – Repair the ruined roof.

- **Special Blocks (Hardwood and Timbered):** Chapter 3 – Build your base to level 5.

- **Stone Furniture:** Chapter 1 – Build you base to level 5.

- **Talaria Accessory (Double Jump):** Chapter 3 – Collect 200 different types of items.

- **Water Crystal:** Chapter 2 – Obtain the crown goowels.

- **Wood Furniture:** Chapter 2 – Build your base to level 5.

Final Fantasy X / X-2 HD Remaster

As you play through this classic RPG, you'll eventually unlock the airship that allows you to travel to new locations. On the travel screen you can input a password to unlock new areas. Here are the passwords to input:

- **Reach Auron's Murasama katana:** MURASAME
- **Reach Rikku's Godhand Celestial Weapon:** GODHAND
- **Reach Rikku's Victorious armour:** VICTORIOUS

Secret Locations.

Once you have the airship you can find some new locations to visit previously. Head to the below X and Y coordinates on the map to find the listed locations.

- **Baaj Temple:** X=11, Y=57
- **Besaid Falls:** X=29, Y=73
- **Mi'ihen Ruins:** X=33, Y=55
- **Omega Ruins:** X=69, Y=33
- **Sanubia Sands:** X=12, Y=41

Go Vacation

How to Play Cloudy Mode on Snow Resort.

To unlock this Mode, first go to the screen where you select the Snow Resort. Then hold R and X while you press A. Don't let go of R and X until the Snow Resort loads. If done correctly you should notice that the area is cloudy.

Hyrule Warriors

How to Unlock Hidden Characters and Weapons

There are stacks of extras to unlock in this awesome action game, and if you complete the following requirements, you will get them all. As you read the below, just remember that we've listed the character first, then the weapon.

- **Ganondorf / Thief's Trident:** Clear square B8 on the Adventure map with an A ranking

- **Impa / Guardian Naginata:** Clear square G11 on the Adventure map with an A ranking

- **King Daphnes / Windfall Sail:** Clear "Reclaiming the Darkness" in Legend Mode

- **Lana / Deku Spear:** Clear "The Sorceress of the Valley" in Legend Mode

- **Lana / Gate of Time:** Clear square A9 on the Adventure map with an A ranking

- **Link / Ancient Spinner:** Clear square C2 on the Adventure map with an A ranking

- **Link / Epona:** Clear square E15 on the Adventure map with an A ranking

- **Link / Fire Rod:** Clear "The Shiekah Tribesmen" in Legend Mode

- **Link / Giant Fountain Fairy:** Clear square H1 on the Adventure map with an A ranking

- **Link / Silver Gauntlets:** Clear square G14 on the Adventure map with an A ranking

- **Linkle / Winged Boots:** Clear square A16 on the Adventure map with an A ranking

- **Marin / Sea Lily Bell:** Clear square E3 on Koholint Island map

- **Medli / Sacred Harp:** Clear square B8 on the Great Sea map

- **Ravio / Wooden Hammer:** Clear square G5 on the Lorule map

- **Skull Kid / Fairy Ocarina:** Clear square C13 on the Adventure map

- **Tetra / Pirate Cutlass:** Clear: "The Search for Cia" in Legend Mode

- **Tingle / Rosy Balloon:** Clear square A12 on the Adventure map

- **Toon Link / Hero's Sword:** Clear square B9 on the Great Sea map

- **Toon Link / Sand Wand:** Clear square D2 on the Grand Travels map with an A ranking

- **Toon Zelda / Protector Sword:** Clear square F11 on the Grand Travels map

- **Twili Midna:** Clear square C6 on the Adventure map

- **Young Link / Fierce Deity Mask:** Clear square G9 on the Adventure map

- **Yuga / Wooden Frame:** Clear square H11 on the Lorule map

- **Zelda / Old Dominion Rod:** Clear square A2 on the Adventure map with an A ranking

- **Zelda / Wind Waker:** Clear square C15 on the Adventure map with an A ranking

Kirby Star Allies

What do you unlock when you beat the game?

You will unlock the Guest Star ???? Star Allies Go mode, as well as The Ultimate Choice mode and the Theater Mode. You will also gain access to two hidden planets in the Far-Flung Starlight Heroes part of the story mode called Ability Planet and Extra Planet Delta.

What do you unlock in this game when you beat Guest Star ???? Star Allies Go mode?

You will get the Jukebox Mode, plus you will unlock difficulty levels 6 and 7 in the Ultimate Choice mode. You will also unlock all currently available Dream Friends for play in this mode.

What do you unlock if you beat The Ultimate Choice mode at level 7?

You get the Soul Melter Difficulty mode.

What do you unlock when you beat The Ultimate Choice mode?

You unlock a range of new characters you can have as allies the next time you play this mode. They are King Dedede, Meta Knight and Bandana Waddle Dee.

Legend of Zelda: Breath of the Wild, The

Amiibo Unlockables Guide

The Legend of Zelda: Breath of the Wild has an interesting connection with many Amiibo figurines. Each day, you can scan any of the below Amiibo and you will receive a reward. Sometimes that will be their Common Drop and other times you will also get some food and materials. But every now and again you will get a Rare Drop, which is extra special. This means it is a good idea to scan whatever Amiibo you have from the below list at least once a day while playing the game so you get the most benefit.

Common Drops:

- **Breath of the Wild Archer Link:** Bows
- **Breath of the Wild Bokoblin:** Clubs
- **Super Smash Bros Zelda or Super Smash Bros Shiek:** Crafting Materials
- **30th Anniversary Wind Waker Link:** Gear
- **Breath of the Wild Horse Rider Link:** Horse Saddles
- **30th Anniversary 8-bit Link:** Rupee Barrels
- **Super Smash Bros Ganondorf:** Rupees and Materials
- **Breath of the Wild Zelda or 30th Anniversary Wind Waker Zelda:** Shields and Cooking Plants
- **30th Anniversary Ocarina of Time Link:** Swords
- **Super Smash Bros Link:** Weapons
- **Breath of the Wild Guardian:** Weapons and Ammo
- **Twilight Princess Wolf Link:** Wolf Link Ally

Rare Drops:

- **Super Smash Bros Link (1st Time only):** Epona
- **30th Anniversary Wind Waker Zelda:** Hero's Shield

- **Breath of the Wild Zelda:** Hylian Shield
- **30th Anniversary 8-bit Link:** Legend of Zelda Tunic
- **30th Anniversary Ocarina of Time Link:** Ocarina of Time Tunic
- **Super Smash Bros Zelda or Super Smash Bros Shiek:** Shiek's Mask
- **Super Smash Bros Ganondorf:** Sword of Six Sages
- **Super Smash Bros Link (2nd Time and Beyond):** Twilight Princess Tunic
- **30th Anniversary Wind Waker Link or Super Smash Bros Toon Link:** Wind Waker Tunic

Bonus Tip:

Be careful when you use the Super Smash Bros. Link Amiibo for the first time. It will give you the awesome horse Epona rare drop straight away. But if you have yet to get far enough into the game to own a stable, then you might lose this special horse – so get the stable first.

Lego Harry Potter Collection

If you go to Diagon Alley and enter Wiseacres Wizarding Equipment you can use these codes to unlock new spells. Just talk to the vendor upstairs:

- **Accio:** VE9VV7
- **Anteoculatia:** QFB6NR
- **Calvorio:** 6DNR6L
- **Colovaria:** 9GJ442
- **Engorgio Skullus:** CD4JLX
- **Entomorphis:** MYN3NB
- **Flipendo:** ND2L7W
- **Glacius:** ERA9DR

- **Herbifors:** H8FTHL
- **Incarcerous:** YEB9Q9
- **Locomotor Mortis:** 2M2XJ6
- **Multicorfors:** JK6QRM
- **Redactum Skullus:** UW8LRH
- **Rictusempra:** 2UCA3M
- **Slugulus Eructo:** U6EE8X
- **Stupefy:** UWDJ4Y
- **Tarentallegra:** KWWQ44
- **Trip Jinx:** YZNRF6

Lego Jurassic World

Pause the game, head to the Extras section, and then select Enter Code. You can then enter in the following cheats.

- **ACU Trooper Male:** 28SPSR
- **Dennis Nedry (Hawaiian):** RAVKRT
- **Dieter Stark:** EKCKLC
- **Dr. Wu:** A3HC7E
- **Indominus Rex Handler:** BX9Z26R
- **InGen Hunter 1:** 8XL359
- **Jeep Driver:** 3FE78R
- **Jimmy Fallon:** 6MKHSG
- **John Hammond (Lost World):** PR2R6Y
- **Jurassic World Veterinarian:** L5AU6Y
- **Minikit Detector:** JYJAFX
- **Studs 2x multiplier:** 5MZ73E

Lego Marvel Superheroes 2

How do I unlock extra characters?

There are two ways to enter cheats in this game. The first is to pause, go to Extras, and then go to Enter Code. Alternatively, you can use the computer that is in Gwenpool's room at the Avenger's Mansion.

- **Ant-Man:** BCR7QJ
- **Baby Groot (Ravager):** QG3VH9
- **Captain Britain:** M68P3L
- **Crimson Dynamo:** CDS278
- **Darkstar:** S947TP
- **Giant-Man:** GAVK9R
- **Grandmaster (Ragnarok):** LBYT59
- **Green Goblin:** XG7SAL
- **Hawkeye:** G6K2VM
- **Hellcow:** NCMJU4
- **Hulkling:** 5G7HFS
- **Loki:** JDNQMV
- **Maestro:** HCE926
- **Militant:** UUTZNC
- **Misty Knight:** BK9B3Y
- **Ragnarok:** HL7L7Y
- **Scarlet Spider:** JD9GQA
- **Songbird:** D6LJ4P
- **Spider-Man UK:** RMADXF
- **Spider-Woman:** CW9BRS

- **Vision (Civil War):** 4U9DAT
- **Vulture (Homecoming):** 7KDY3L
- **Winter Soldier:** 8KD3F6

Lego Movie 2 Videogame

At any time while playing, you can pause the game and enter in one a code through the menu. Unless you are getting studs, you will get a relic. To then open it, you need to head to one of the in-game shops.

Character Relic Codes (Purple Relics)

- H29V4E
- CK3GR7
- NHCBRC
- THSS1T
- QHN4KB
- PC7B52
- MSEGWC

Item Relic Codes (Green Relics)

- ZLWEV4
- V76RFB
- RUL4LU
- 1ZCPYG
- VLNM9B
- 7XJP73

Construction Relic Codes (Blue Relics)

- KEFWX4
- DT98BK

- V8K72L

- BK21FE

- DR8CEE

- PPLFWD

Rare Relic Codes (Gold & Red)

- FR0MTT

- FCRL55

- R3TJU8

Stud Unlock Codes (2000 Studs per code)

- EK5P48

- 5KCT38

- K6DFM6

- U505AD

- XPYJNX

- NAUXRU

- SLBJKK

- PH9NFT

- 4VVXPR

- J3A2VF

Lego Ninjago Movie Video Game

How to Unlock Extra Characters.

Like most of the Lego games, through the main menu you can find an area where you can type in codes. We've found a few codes that can unlock extra characters for you to play. Here they are:

- **Ceremonial Robes Nya:** 8755Q9
- **Garmadon In Pajamas:** LLPQ6X
- **Highschool Cole:** SMMNCC
- **Highschool Jay:** XVTULS
- **Highschool Zane:** 5NHRS5
- **Polybag Lloyd:** H7HGT3
- **Mystery Character:** EFZ2XR
- **Sushi Chef:** KU92UG

Lego The Incredibles

If you want to unlock special cheats in this game, you need to find the rare red bricks. So, where are they?

Red Brick #1: Classic Mode – In the top right corner of Outer Municiberg. Unlock Spot by building the tree house, then dig up the dirt in front of the tree.

Red Brick #2: Pickup Detector – Get Flik by doing the Family Build in the centre of Urbem Heights. Dig up the dirt in front and behind the cart, then turn the crank.

Red Brick #3: Destroy on Contact – Do the Family Build at the empty space near the construction site on the left side of the Financial District. When you get Russell, head to the front yard of the house. Dig up the bricks and use them to build a path up to the attic. Smash all the glowing objects and then rebuild them.

Red Brick #4: Edna Mode... Mode – At the Docks, find the Family Build and create the Monster's Inc. facility. Smash everything inside so you can build the monster, then press the red button.

Red Brick #5: Fast Interact – Do the Family Build in the top right corner of the Residential District. Then go to Imagination Land, find the lava pool and hop across the blue spots to the middle button. Then build the chess piece.

Red Brick #6: Invincibility – There's a Family Build in the top right corner of the Waterfront District. After you create the racetrack, start racing and complete the track in less than 1min 40seconds.

Red Brick #7: Stud Magnet – Go to the centre of the Tourist District and do the Family Build to create Pizza Planet. There is a rocket behind it with a grapple point, which can use to get inside. Then use the wheel on the grabber machine.

Red Brick #8: x10 Studs Multiplier – In the top left corner of the Industrial District there is a Family Build that creates Wall-E. His laser can cut open the huge truck where you can break the gold objects. Then break the shelf to build a switch.

Red Brick #9: Swing Mode – Use the Family Build at the Waterfront to unlock Dory, as well as a reef that sinks underwater. Use Dory to swim underwater and break up the blue Lego blocks to open the clam.

Codes.

If you pause the game, then select the Extras option from the menu, you can enter the following codes:

- **Gamma Jack:** G1MHR7
- **Edna Mode (Juniors):** BRAB1R

Lego City Undercover

Extra Characters.

To enter the following codes, head to the EXTRAS option in the menu and type in the desired code.

- **Baseball Player:** 5MCPHUL
- **Classic Alien:** 8JQBUKE
- **Drakonas:** TQ53GQB
- **Roman Soldier:** B2L8U2E
- **Sushi Chef:** KU92UG

Lego Worlds

Enter the following codes through the Main Menu:

- **All building bricks:** BR1CK5

- **All doors and windows:** F1XTRS

- **Getaway Car from LEGO City:** BG7DWK

- **Lance's Driller from Nexo Knights:** XP3BN2

- **Lock & Roller from Nexo Knights:** LY9C8M

- **Pizza Van from LEGO City:** U98BR2

- **Police Car from LEGO City:** P42FJ6

Mario + Rabbids: Kingdom Battle

Important Tips.

1. When you target an enemy, it tells you the chances of your shot hitting. Don't take too many chances and go for the shots with the highest percentage chance of success.

2. You can reduce the chance of your enemy making a successful shot by using cover. But make sure you move around, or your enemy will destroy the cover and leave you vulnerable.

3. Keep an eye on each of the new powers and abilities you earn. They take a while to recharge after use, but as soon as they are ready again, you should activate them.

4. Don't be overly concerned about winning in the correct amount of turns. It's more important to just win and progress. Later on, you can come back to beat your record.

5. There is a mid-boss and main boss in each level, and they are the toughest fights. Make sure you go in prepared and with everything charged.

6. It's important not to rush. Take your time planning each play, and don't forget helpful abilities like Dash and Team Jumps.

Mario Kart 8 Deluxe

Unlockables

- **Gold Mario:** If you place first in all of the 12 Cups on the 200cc difficulty, you will be able to turn Metal Mario into the highly sought-after Gold Mario.

- **Gold Glider:** Collect a total of 5,000 coins.

- **Gold Standard Kart:** Place first in every single Grand Prix Cup with a single star on both the 150cc and Mirror modes.

- **Gold Tires:** Beat every single Staff Ghost in the Time Trial mode on the 150cc setting.

- **Earn a New Part:** Every time you collect 30 coins in the Grand Prix mode, you will unlock a new part for your karts. These regular parts are randomly selected, so part of the fun is seeing what you will get next.

Choose a Season

When you are choosing the Animal Crossing track to race upon, you can actually select the season you are driving through. As you select the track, hold down one of the following buttons to decide on the season you want:

- **Spring:** L

- **Summer:** R

- **Autumn:** ZL

- **Winter:** ZR

How to get a Turbo Boost at the start of a race.

If you want to get your race off to a fast start, hold down the accelerator at the exact moment that the "2" begins to fade on the race starting lights. If you time it perfectly, you will start with a bonus nitro boost.

Best Kart and Character Combo.

In order to get the fastest lap times in the mighty Mario Kart, you'll have to use a certain combination of character and kart. And then drive perfectly! Heavy characters have the highest top speed, but you can't make one mistake as their acceleration is terrible. You can try and balance it out with better grip of course, and also try to learn all the best trick, drift-boost and shortcut locations. Here is a good combo:

- **Character:** Any Level 3 Heavy (Bowser, Wario, Donkey Kong Jr. or Morton)

- **Kart:** Pipeframe, Blue Falcon and Streetle (best balance of speed and friction)

- **Tyres:** Slick

- **Glider:** Anything

Mario Tennis Aces

How to Unlock New Characters.

Mario Tennis Aces takes a different approach to unlocking than previous Nintendo games. You need to play online tournaments to get new characters, with a new character available each month. For July, that character was Blooper, a squid from Splatoon.

How to Unlock New Courts.

There are five courts to unlock and you get one for finishing each of the game's five areas in Adventure Mode. Once unlocked, these courts can be customised so you can have some extra obstacles to the fun. Eventually you will end up with:

- Marina Stadium (Night)

- Marina Stadium

- Bask Ruins

- Piranha Plant Forest

- Mirage Mansion

- Snowfall Mountain
- Savage Sea
- Volcano Court

Marvel Ultimate Alliance: Black Order

Achieve these goals to unlock the bonuses.

- **Star 1 on the Save Menu:** Beat the game
- **Star 2 on the Save Menu:** Beat the game on Superior
- **Star 3 on the Save Menu:** Beat the game on Ultimate
- **Star 4 on the Save Menu:** Complete the Enhancement Grid
- **Star 5 on the Save Menu:** Get every star in the five Infinity Rifts
- **Elektra Character:** Clear the "Bad Business" Infinity Trial
- **Loki Character:** Clear the "Defeat Ebony Maw & 4 Bosses" Infinity Trial
- **Magneto Character:** Clear the "Defeat Klaw & 2 Bosses" Infinity Trial
- **Thanos Character:** Unlock Superior Difficulty and the Lambda infinity trials, then clear the The Black Order Infinity Trial
- **Superior difficulty:** Beat the story on any difficulty
- **Ultimate Difficulty, New Rift Trials and Fifth Ability Rank:** Beat Superior Difficulty mode.

Mega Man 11

End Game Bonuses.

When you finish the game, two cheats will become available to buy in the shop for 3000 bolts each. You can get:

- **Awakening Chip:** Infinite Weapon Energy
- **Cooling System:** Infinite Double Gear Time

Extra Lives.

Make your way to Dr. Light's lab and buy a Mystery Tank. Then head to Acid Man's stage and when you come across the first spider, shoot it twice with the Mega Buster. If you do this correctly, mini-spider bots should appear. Once they have landed, open the menu and choose your Mystery Tank. All the spiders will then turn into extra lives!

New Super Mario Bros. Deluxe

Flagpole Secrets.

Did you know that if you jump on the flagpole at the end of a level and the last two numbers on the countdown clock are the same, then not only do you get a fireworks display, but Toad will pop up and give you a free item. Here is what you can get:

- **Fire Flower:** Last two numbers are 33 or 44

- **Ice Flower:** Last two numbers are 55

- **Star:** Last two numbers are 88 or 99

- **Super Acorn:** Last two numbers are 77

- **Super Mushroom:** Last two numbers are 11 or 22

- **Tiny Mushroom:** Last two numbers are 66

Play as Nabbit in Single Player.

Sick of Mario and Luigi? You can actually go through the single player as Nabbit if you like. Hold down ZL when you are selecting a stage and Nabbit will turn up instead of Luigi. Don't worry, Luigi returns once you finish the stage. Bizarrely, if you try this trick on the final Superstar Road level, it won't be Nabbit, but your Mii character, that appears when you start.

Propeller Hat and Penguin Suit.

To get these power-ups from New Super Mario Bros. Wii, you must first finish the game and unlock the Superstar Road. You can then find these items in the Toad Houses and use them in any level.

Overcooked 2

How to Unlock New Levels.

If you nail certain combos – which means serving meals in the order they are listed – you begin to unlock bonus Kevin levels. There are different criteria based on whether you are playing with a friend or by yourself, and here they are:

- **Kevin 1: Level 1-3:** Get a combo of 2 (solo or co-op)

- **Kevin 2: Level 2-2:** Get a combo of 3 (solo) or 5 (co-op)

- **Kevin 3: Level 2-4:** Get a score of 600 (solo) or 1,000 (co-op)

- **Kevin 4: Level 3-1:** Get a score of 450 (solo) or 1,100 (co-op)

- **Kevin 5: Level 4-3:** Get a combo of 4 (solo) or 5 (co-op)

- **Kevin 6: Level 4-5:** Get a score of 400 (solo) or 500 (co-op)

- **Kevin 7: Level 5-5:** Get a combo of 5 (solo) or 8 (co-op)

- **Kevin 8: Level 6-4:** Get a combo of 5 (solo) or 7 (co-op)

Pokémon Mystery Dungeon: Rescue Team DX

At the title screen you can enter passwords. When you enter one, it will unlock a mission that, if you complete, will reward you with a Pokémon.

- **Beautifly:** CNTSN2F1

- **Chingling:** R6T1XSH5

- **Clefairy:** 8TT498W8

- **Dragonair:** HK5R3N47

- **Larvitar:** 5JSMNWF0

- **Mantyke:** MF0K5CCN

- **Mareep:** 991Y5K47

- **Misdreavus:** 5K0K0K2K

- **Rhyhorn:** R8Y48QXR

- **Roselia:** K762CJWF

- **Sableye:** 91SR2H5J

- **Slowpoke:** 6Y6SNWHF

- **Smoochum:** 92JMR48W

- **Togetic:** MHJR625M

- **Wailmer:** 0R5H76XQ

Pokémon Quest

Here are five quick steps to get you started in this free-to-play game.

1. **Pick the right starter:** At the beginning you must choose between Charmander, Squirtle, Bulbasaur, Pikachu and Eevee. Choose one with attributes that differ from Pokémon you're likely to catch early in the game. We opt for Charmander.

2. **Complete daily quests/challenges:** This is the quickest way to get the PM Tickets you need to progress. Look for the easiest challenges in the quest hub and do those first.

3. **Don't miss your rewards:** When you finish a challenge, don't forget to grab the reward. Just look for the exclamation mark (!) in the quest menu.

4. **Daily visit:** Make sure you sign-in each day and grab your daily rewards if you want to level quickly.

5. **Equip Power Stones:** The higher your Pokémon's level, the more Power Stones it can hold, giving you more stat boosts. This is important for winning early battles.

Pokémon Sword & Shield

The weather in this game is randomised, but it's also based on the date based in your system settings. If you change the date in your system settings, it will change the weather in the game, which can help you find Pokémon that only come out in certain conditions. Here's the settings you need to get the weather you want:

- **Clear** = 1/5/2020

- **Sunny** = 1/7/2020

- **Cloudy** = 1/3/2020

- **Rain** = 1/10/2020

- **Thunderstorm** = 1/11/2020

- **Snow** = **1**/12/2020

- **Hail** = 1/2/2020 (once you have four badges)

- **Sandstorm** = 1/4/2020 (once you have four badges)

- **Fog** = 1/6/2020 (only works after you have defeated the Champion

Pokken Tournament DX

Go to the Pause Menu when you are on the World Map and there will be a bonus code option. Type in these codes to get the bonus:

- **Hamburger Hat (Female):** USBXKG8X4GLG

- **Hamburger Hat (Male):** H5D9YZFETCQZ

- **Old Leather Jacket (Female):** NQLMEMRGX37X

- **Old Leather Jacket (Male):** 6GSSALLDM9RL

- **Pokémon T Shirts (Female):** J7XEEQLYNDMT

- **Pokémon T Shirts (Male):** TC2JY22VBQUU

Snake Pass

8-Bit Costumes: If you manage to collect all the Wisps and Gatekeeper Coins in the game, you will unlock retro 8-bit costumers for both Noodle and Doodle.

Snake Vision: Once you have finished the game, you will unlock a powerful ability called Snake Vision. If you click in the right stick, you will now be able to tell where all the collectables are in a level using this power.

Sonic Forces

Create Additional Avatars.

When you first start the game, you can create a custom character for the story campaign, but only one. This is really annoying, especially as there are many different animal-specific missions to play during the game. The good news is that when you finish the main story and watch all the credits, the option to make extra characters appears. You can then go to the Avatar menu in options to swap between them.

Sonic Mania

Level Select.

If you want to be able to choose any level to play, you must do the following button combos: as the game is loading up, hold down the B and the Y buttons until the "press any button" message comes up.

Unlock the True Final Boss.

First you must play as Sonic. Then your must have all seven Chaos Emeralds before you finish the Titanic Monarch Act 2 level. If done correctly, when you beat the normal boss in that level, Sonic will be teleported to a final face off against the true boss.

Unlockables

- **Super Peel Out:** 1 medal
- **Insta-Shield:** 6 medals
- **&Knuckles Mode:** 11 medals
- **Debug Mode:** 16 medals
- **Mean Bean:** 21 medals

- **D.A. Garden:** 26 medals
- **All Blue Spheres Stages:** 32 medals

Splatoon! 2

Unlockable Weapons

Once you reach a certain level in the multiplayer mode, you can unlock new weapons to purchase at Ammo Knights. Here is the order you get them:

- **Reach Level 2:** Splattershot
- **Reach Level 4:** Tentatek Splattershot
- **Reach Level 4:** Splat Charger
- **Reach Level 4:** Splat Dualies
- **Reach Level 4:** Splat Roller
- **Reach Level 5:** Blaster
- **Reach Level 5:** Slosher
- **Reach Level 6:** Aerospray MG
- **Reach Level 7:** Carbon Roller
- **Reach Level 8:** Heavy Splatling
- **Reach Level 9:** N-Zap '85
- **Reach Level 10:** Octobrush
- **Reach Level 10:** Splattershot Pro
- **Reach Level 11:** Enperry Splat Dualies
- **Reach Level 12:** Krak-On Splat Roller
- **Reach Level 13:** Rapid Blaster
- **Reach Level 14:** .52 Gal
- **Reach Level 15:** Splatterscope

- **Reach Level 15:** Tri-Slosher
- **Reach Level 16:** Firefin Splat Charger
- **Reach Level 17:** Jet Squelcher
- **Reach Level 18:** L-3 Nozzlenose
- **Reach Level 19: L**una Blaster
- **Reach Level 20:** Dynamo Roller
- **Reach Level 20:** E-Liter 4K
- **Reach Level 21:** .96 Gal
- **Reach Level 22:** Goo Tuber
- **Reach Level 23:** Mini Splatling
- **Reach Level 24:** Flingza Roller
- **Reach Level 25:** Firefin Splatterscope
- **Reach Level 25:** Splash-o-Matic
- **Reach Level 26:** Dapple Dualies
- **Reach Level 27:** Custom Blaster
- **Reach Level 28:** Aerospray RG
- **Reach Level 29: H-3** Nozzlenose
- **Reach Level 30:** Clash Blaster
- **Reach Level 30:** E-Liter 4K Scope

Super Bomberman R

What happens when you finish the Story Mode?

Once you have finished the Story Mode, you will unlock in the shop Golem Bomber, Karaoke Bomber, Magnet Bomber, Phantom Bomber and Plasma Bomber. However, you will then need to spend 5,000 gems on each of them for them to become playable. If you manage to finish Story Mode with three-stars on every level, you will also unlock

Pretty Bomber. However, she will cost you 30,000 gems to make playable.

Unlockables

- **Level Select:** Beat the story mode

- **Golem Bomber:** Beat the story mode and buy for 5000 gems in the shop

- **Karaoke Bomber:** Beat the story mode and buy for 5000 gems in the shop

- **Magnet Bomber:** Beat the story mode and buy for 5000 gems in the shop

- **Phantom Bomber:** Beat the story mode and buy for 5000 gems in the shop

- **Plasma Bomber:** Beat the story mode and buy for 5000 gems in the shop

- **Pretty Bomber:** If you get three stars on every world, you can buy her for 30000 gems in the shop

Super Mario Odyssey

Unlock Three New Kingdoms.

Did you know there are three secret kingdoms to unlock in this awesome game? They all involve finishing the game, and then depending on what other achievements have been met, they become available.

They are:

- **Mushroom Kingdom:** Beat the final boss on the Moon.

- **Dark Side:** Beat the final boss on the Moon and find 250 moons.

- **Darker Side:** Beat the final boss on the Moon and on Dark Side and find 500 moons.

Amiibo Bonuses.

If you tap an Amiibo figurine while playing Super Mario Odyssey, you will unlock the below:

- **Highlight Purple Coins on-screen (not on your map):** Any Bowser amiibo

- **Life-Up Heart:** Any Peach amiibo

- **Random coins or bonus hearts:** Any amiibo or amiibo card

- **Temporary Invincibility (30 sec):** Any Mario amiibo

Super Mario Party

Unlockables

Gold Oar: Complete the five different routes in the River Survival Mode. Then talk to Birdo in the plaza and when she asks you a question, choose Gold Oar.

Challenge Road Mode: Unlock every minigame.

Diddy Kong: First you must clear the Chestnut Forest (World 2) in Challenge Road, then talk to him in the plaza.

Donkey Kong: First clear three different River Survival courses, then talk to him in the plaza.

Kamek's Tantalizing Tower Board: Simply play all the other boards in the game at least once.

Pom Pom: First you must clear the Salty Sea (World 5) in Challenge Road, then talk to her in the plaza.

Yooka-Laylee

Here are few tips that we picked up while playing this great platformer.

Don't Get Distracted: Sometimes you will see stuff that looks hard to get to. Don't waste too much time on it. Just keep moving as you will quickly earn a new ability that will help you get there.

Get All the Quills: Every time you see a quill, make sure you pick it up. This is what you will use to buy new skills.

Stuck on a Puzzle? If so, try some of your other abilities. You get a lot in this game, and the one you are supposed to use is not always obvious.

Listen Out: Lots of hidden items make sounds, so you need to listen out for them to know that they are nearby. For example, this is how you can find ghosts.

Hunter: Focus on getting the Hunter tonic as soon as you can by finding two health or battery extenders. This plays a sound when a rare item is nearby: very handy.

Yoshi's Crafted World

Amiibo Costumes.

There are a few bonus costumes you can get in Yoshi's Crafted World by scanning an amiibo while playing the game. Here are the amiibos that work and what they give you.

- **Blue Yarn Yoshi:** Scan the Blue Yarn Yoshi amiibo

- **Bowser:** Scan any Bowser amiibo

- **Green Yarn Yoshi:** Scan the normal Green Yarn Yoshi or the Mega Yarn Yoshi

- **Koopa Troopa:** Scan the Koopa Troopa amiibo

- **Luigi:** Scan any Luigi amiibo

- **Mario:** Scan any Mario amiibo

- **Peach:** Scan any Peach amiibo

- **Pink Yarn Yoshi:** Scan the Pink Yarn Yoshi amiibo

- **Toad:** Scan the Toad amiibo

- **Yarn Poochy:** Scan the Yarn Poochy amiibo

- **Yoshi:** Scan any plastic Yoshi amiibo

- **Amiibo Box:** Scan any other amiibo

MORE TO COME

We're busy working away on big guides for the launch of the Xbox Series X and the PlayStation 5, the next generation of consoles. We'll also look to update this guide to the Nintendo Switch as more great games arrive over the coming months and years.

To make sure you're on top of every release from Old Mate Media, make sure you sign-up to the newsletter.

We also have plenty of other great books to explore. Make sure you check out our sci-fi series **Adam X**, which is very much inspired by a mix of video games like Mass Effect and movies like Star Wars. If you're a parent, we also have a stack of great picture books, cookbooks and activities guides, too.

Just head to www.oldmatemedia.com

OUT NOW

ULTIMATE AT HOME
ACTIVITIES FOR KIDS

150+ FUN GAMES

KATE & CHRIS STEAD